"I could not put this book down! Not only is she an excellent writer, Luz Canino-Baker is a role model of living an intentional life. Luz's story and the tools she offers are truly valuable, easy to grasp, and at the same time profound. Delightful to read, I will be recommending this book and Luz's method to my clients and students again and again."

—Dr. Tracey L. Cantarutti, executive coach and leadership development consultant, TLC Leadership Options, Inc.

"Luz Canino-Baker's book is a gift to readers who desire to be the owners of their lives and destiny. Her work is an easy-to-follow Life GPS using practical concepts, real life stories, and powerful exercises."

—Murray A. Mann, author and principal of Global Diversity Solutions Group LLC

"*Designing Your Life Plan* by Luz Canino-Baker is like having a personal coach and mentor sitting across from you. You will explore concrete ways that you can evaluate what is going right in your life and what you want different. Ms. Canino-Baker reaches across the page and asks you questions that will make you stand up and take action!"

—Helene Van Manen, master coach and founder of *www.RetreatCoaches.com*

DESIGNING YOUR LIFE PLAN

Breaking Your Limiting Routines to Step into Intentional Living

Luz Canino-Baker

Writers of the Round Table Press
PO Box 511, Highland Park, Il 60035
www.roundtablecompanies.com

Publisher: *Corey Michael Blake*
Lead Editor: *Aaron Hierholzer*
Directoress of Happiness: *Erin Cohen*
Director of Author Services: *Kristin Westberg*
Facts Keeper: *Mike Winicour*
Cover Design: *Analee Paz*
Print and Digital Interior Design: *Sunny DiMartino*
Proofreading: *Rita Hess*
Last Looks: *Sunny DiMartino*
Print and Digital Post Production: *Sunny DiMartino*

Printed in the United States of America

First Edition: November 2013
10 9 8 7 6 5 4 3 2 1

Library of Congress Cataloging-in-Publication Data
Canino-Baker, Luz.
Designing your life plan: breaking your limiting routines to step into intentional
living / Luz Canino-Baker.—1st ed. p. cm.
ISBN Paperback 978-1-939418-46-3
ISBN Digital 978-1-939418-47-0
Library of Congress Control Number: 2013952377

RTC Publishing is an imprint of Writers of the Round Table, Inc.
Writers of the Round Table Press and the RTC Publishing logo
are trademarks of Writers of the Round Table, Inc.

Contents

Introduction

Do you talk about, dream about, and desire a life that you don't have today? Are you always meaning to start toward the life you want, only to find yourself stuck, skipping like a broken record? Do you sometimes stop and wonder if there's more to life than the stale-seeming reality you exist in for most of the day?

I was there before I wrote my very first Life Plan, before I made it my profession to help other people build theirs. The fact that you are reading this book means you're probably ready to figure out how to reach the life you want. As you turn each page, you will begin a self-discovery journey that ends with your own Life Plan, designed by you, for you. We're about to set out on a mission to bring your dreams and hopes to paper and work out a roadmap for your life, one that specifies what you want to aim for in the next five years. I am a big believer in the concept that taking things out of our heads and putting them down on paper gives clarity and direction. By the end of this book, I hope you'll be a believer in this, too.

I have been a life coach since early 2002, before coaching became popular. I became a coach because I saw people changing their lives when they took time to clearly identify their hopes and dreams and form a plan for their lives. I saw people who lived with fear conquer those fears; I saw people who were hindered by negative thoughts emerge as confident men and women who took bold actions in their lives. Seeing this made me aware that we all have much more in common than we think, which means we understand each other and can help each other. To me, that's what life coaching is all about, and I absolutely love it.

Before I wrote my first Life Plan, my life was unexamined and filled with routines. But my Life Plan challenges me to examine my routines and keeps me headed in the right direction. I want to get you to that point, too.

This book has been about three years in the making. When I started coaching, I didn't know that I wanted to write a book. In fact, a book was not in my initial five-year plan! However, as I coached clients, I found that I needed a tool to demonstrate how to carry out the recommendations I was giving them. This book was written to serve that need and then evolved into a guide for anyone who wants to live intentionally, whether a client of mine or not.

First and foremost, I want to thank God, who taught me what fatherly love is by always being present and showing me my path.

Second, I want to thank my wonderful husband, Don, for believing in my life dreams from the moment we met. The fact that you believed in my career domain and had the architect build me a home office before I realized my career as a life coach spoke volumes to me and inspired my commitment to my own dreams.

I want to thank my daughter Michelle for the endless hours she dedicated to editing the early versions of the book. I know you were busy with your own work, but I could have never completed this book without your keen eyes.

And next, I want to thank all three of my wonderful children—Steven, Katherine, and Michelle—for allowing me to share my life with my clients as I was raising the three of you as a single mother. I know that you probably didn't understand why I was always on the phone or meeting people, but I hope I have inspired you to help others reach their life dreams and have helped you live your life with intention.

I am in awe of the work that Round Table Companies did to make this a book that I am proud to put in the marketplace. In particular, I want to acknowledge Aaron, my primary editor, for his attention to detail, his skill in taking my thoughts and shaping them into beautiful words that conveyed what I wanted to say. To the rest of the team, especially Corey and Erin, who served to keep Aaron and I on point—I always found your input insightful and inspiring.

Chapter 1

The First Step:
Break Your Routines

▶▶ Most of us step out of bed each morning on autopilot. We shuffle to the kitchen, put on the coffee pot, shower, floss, and throw together some sandwiches for the kids—whatever it is we do to prepare for the day. We don't think about what we're doing. We just do it.

So? you may be wondering. *What's wrong with that? Routines help give my life order. They help me stay on track.*

But there is a problem, because routines don't just rule our mornings—they rule our entire lives. Most of our actions throughout the day, whether at home, at school, or at work, are part of a deeply ingrained and interrelated set of routines. These routines become helpful and comfortable indeed. And when something threatens the little comfort zone we've created through these routines, we can get defensive and protective.

Of course, routines aren't inherently bad for you. They can add predictability and security to life. Some routines are positive; they reduce stress and help us live productive lives. If you're in boot camp, the routines you're learning could even ensure your survival on the battlefield. But when we sink too deeply into the repetitive patterns of life, it's all too easy to wake up one day and wonder, *Where on earth did the years go?*

If any of this sounds familiar, it's likely that you've allowed yourself to get too comfortable in your routines and that you're being held back from stepping up to your full potential. The antidote is intentional living—living with a plan. I see it work wonders with my clients on a weekly basis.

By the time you finish this book, you'll have built out your own personalized Life Plan, but before we start on any of that, it's vital that we do some deep self-exploration. The comfort of routines can so easily lure us from the path to true happiness—we pass up opportunities and shrug off the burden of new experiences in favor of the security of what we're used to. So in this chapter, we're going to look at how routines shape us, from childhood to our careers, and how we can start breaking free. This is the first step on your journey toward a full Life Plan.

Let's go all the way back to where a ton of our routines originated: childhood and school days.

Routines at Home and School

The truly lucky among us grow up with a mother and father to feed us, change our diapers, and comfort us when we shed a tear. Our parents provided for our every need and protected us at every turn, warding off all the dangers of life. Thus, as infants, we were introduced to our very first comfort zone.

But as all mother birds know, comfort zones and complete dependence can't last forever. As soon as baby birds are old enough, the mother shoves the young out of the nest—it's the only way they'll ever learn to fly. For human parents, pushing children out into the real world can be a painful process, but they know we must be weaned from our comfortable and protected lives.

I was five years old when I was first pushed from the nest.

One September day, my mom woke me up early and put me in a nice dress and some fancy socks with ruffles around the ankle. My mother, too, was done up in nice clothes and makeup that morning, and the scent of her perfume clued me in to the fact that we were going somewhere special. It's very likely I thought we were going to church.

But it wasn't a Sunday, and I soon found out that this was to be my first day in kindergarten. That morning, my mother and I walked, hand in hand, to the elementary school just down the street from our house. When we entered the classroom, we were still holding hands, and I didn't quite know what was going on. I saw a lot of other boys and girls who were beginning to take their seats. Only when my mother let go of my hand did I understand the situation. She told me I had to stay and that she would see me later. I immediately threw myself down on the ground of that classroom and cried, my feet kicking futilely in the air.

As the kindergarten teacher tried to distract the children, who were now all staring at me, my mother took me out into the hallway.

"It's okay, Luz," she cooed.

I'd calmed down a bit, but I couldn't speak. I just stared at her, sniffling.

Mom reached into her bulky purse and pulled out a gleaming quarter. "You can have this to yourself if you stay and be a good girl, Luz," she said.

That was all it took. To my five-year-old self, a quarter was a princely sum. I gave Mom a hug, took the coin in my palm, brushed myself off, and walked bravely back to the classroom and my seat. Little did I know that this day marked the abrupt and final shattering of the familiar home routine I'd known all my life.

School is often the first place where we feel we are truly outside of our comfort zones. We find ourselves among strange children and unfamiliar adults. After that first traumatic day, however, it didn't take long for a new set of routines to crop up. I'd left the comfort of being with a parent all day and now needed a new, predictable regimen to calm me. With the anxiety of my mom leaving me that first day still fresh in my young mind, I fell into habits and reassuring patterns.

The routines we adopt in school are part of growing up. We learn to be at class on time, to turn in homework, to study before tests, and to follow rules. We learn about deadlines for the first time and the series of events around them: the anticipation, the bout of hard work just before the due date, and the relief once we meet it. We feel the ebb and flow of the academic year, the joy of approaching summer and the dread of the back-to-school season. Encouraged by parents and teachers, we learn to walk the predictable walk through the year, without questioning the monotony of our daily lives.

By the time we get to high school, we are already conditioned to follow certain routines. We wake up, go to school, come home, finish homework, hang out with friends, eat, sleep, and so on. Each day has a similar series of events. I realize that these routines are not the same for everyone, particularly for those whose childhood experiences are harmed by alcoholism, drugs, or sexual abuse. Nonetheless, routines can take over their lives just as easily, although they are often painful ones.

Without the will to exert any energy or spend any time on changing ourselves, the routines established in school persist. It is much easier to keep repeating what's familiar and safe, even if that safety is merely perceived.

Routines in the Workplace

When we finally reach graduation and transition from school to work, one set of routines ends and another begins. Many people start to get bogged down and held back by routines in this professional stage of life. The stakes are higher in the workplace than they were before; it is a completely new environment, and here we travel alone. And, this stage of life doesn't seem to have a clear endpoint: few people accept their first job with an idea of how they will eventually leave the workforce.

Despite the challenges, post-school adulthood can be an incredible time to shatter all our limiting routines and carve out the path to the life we really want. In fact, many of us start out with that intention. *This is temporary*, we tell ourselves. *I won't stay here long.* But then life creeps in and lifestyles evolve, debt lures its ugly head, and we're caught—trapped once again in a complex set of routines.

Most workplaces are driven by structure and rules: start times, break times, end times, dress codes, protocols, and hierarchies. Financial incentives are used to encourage participation and stir competition. Procedure and policy manuals state some of the rules but leave many unspoken. And as with any game, there are consequences for not playing by the rules—even if we don't have the full playbook. Our bosses direct us to embrace the procedures they have established. The very function of the workplace is to make us responsible for carrying out various tasks and routines.

Here's what happens to many of us when the routines of the workplace drive our life. We start out very optimistic, and we begin to adapt to the routines of our job. We do the assigned tasks, go to all our meetings, collect our paychecks, and all seems well. But as time progresses, that routine doesn't seem to match what we really want out of life, so we start taking more professional risks: we seek promotions or we switch jobs. But we soon find that everyone around us is doing the same thing, and we are constantly competing to keep our job or secure the next one. Meanwhile, our lifestyle has changed to meet the income levels we can now afford—or, in far too many cases, that we *can't* afford. It's like we're all playing a life-size game of Monopoly, throwing the dice again and again, circling the board endlessly, with no end until a winner emerges and all others are left bankrupt.

When we realize we're stuck in such a rut, we usually start seeking help—whether it's from a life coach or a self-help book. But regardless of what our aspirations for life are, the first requirement is that we shatter the limiting routines in our lives.

Breaking Free of Routines

As you can see, routines—both the beneficial ones and those that limit us—mark every phase of our lives. But if we are to truly become the best version of ourselves possible, it's essential that we stop the endless cycle. We must wake up, stomp a foot to the floor, and take a hard look at *why* we're doing what we do and figure out whether it's helping us get where the deepest, most honest part of us wants to go.

In the time I've spent working with clients and observing people, I've identified three things that can help us jump out of our systemized, habit-driven lives: our *mentors*, our *beliefs and passions*, and *effective goal setting*. In the following pages, we'll take a look at how each one helps us move toward our dreams. You'll need to have all three at your disposal as you move through this book and build your Life Plan.

Mentors

In high school, we're saddled with abundant routines, but these years are also the time when we meet many of the overseers of our future—the teachers, the counselors, and the social workers whose job it is to guide us. These mentors can often help break us out of the patterns we've grown accustomed to, especially the ones that are holding us back.

One of my first mentors was Mr. MacDonald, a school counselor with a reputation for being something of a hippy. It was Mr. MacDonald who first advised me against my youthful dream of ditching school to be a flight attendant. (I got as far as sending in an application, but the man who followed up at my home was surprised to find an eager sixteen-year-old candidate.) When Mr. MacDonald heard about my plan, he didn't give the response I expected based on his hippy persona: "It's all cool, man." Instead, he reached into his filing cabinet and pulled out a set of college applications. "Fill these out tonight," he said, "and I'll help you get them mailed."

As I look back at Mr. MacDonald, I see how it sometimes takes an intermediary to point out how routines are clouding our vision of the world around us. And never was this truer than with another of my high school mentors, Mrs. Espinoza. She was the social worker at my high school, and she'd come to school every week to have what she called "rap sessions" with me and about ten other girls. Mrs. Espinoza got us to talk about our lives and our routines in these sessions, and she would often take us on weekend daytrips to different neighborhoods of Chicago—from downtown to uptown to Chinatown. The other girls and I would meet her at the school on Saturday morning and file onto the city bus that would take us toward our destination.

The first of these trips was a huge break from my typical

routine. I had never been on a bus before, outside of one trip to the doctor with my mother. Back then, my family walked everywhere, which meant I didn't even know how large the city of Chicago really was. To me, it consisted of the few blocks that surrounded my home. But these trips with Mrs. Espinoza stretched my horizons and opened up a new world to me.

One day, Mrs. Espinoza took us to Chinatown, and I can still recall the new sights and smells that captivated me immediately. The rhythm of a foreign language, the tantalizing smells of cooking food, small shops filled with objects I'd never seen before, and the faces of Chinese people (a rare sight in my community)—it all mesmerized me. I especially loved the colorful paper umbrellas, like the ones we now see in fancy drinks. I felt like I was in a strange land, albeit one that had existed just outside the bounds of my everyday sphere. Mrs. Espinoza didn't have to take us on weekend trips or use her personal time to expose us to new things and shatter our limiting view of the city. But without her, I wouldn't have had those incredible experiences.

I'd also become a Cubs fan in high school, and now that Mrs. Espinoza had taught me how to take the bus to Wrigleyville, I could enjoy the long, slow bus ride from the south side to the north side and see my favorite team play. Breaking from the old habit of staying in my own neighborhood gave me many exhilarating experiences at Wrigley Field.

In this way, mentors and guides can open our minds and break our routines—and it doesn't just happen while we're kids. Our professional lives, as we talked about earlier, can feel like little more than a complex system of routines and rules; and at the office, we don't easily find people who have a vested interest in guiding us, as a parent or teacher would. And yet, even in the workplace, it's possible to find people who willingly devote time and energy to make you a better human being. Though our bosses and colleagues are not there to coddle us or lead us down life's path, some do break through the routines and offer real inspiration; they teach us, direct us, and give us opportunities to demonstrate our strengths.

For three years early in my career, I worked as a file clerk at a bank, and it was the most monotonous job you could imagine. Every day, thousands of checks would arrive at my desk in black bins, having been sorted by account number. I was responsible for examining each check to ensure it was good and then filing it in a long metal cabinet. There were about ten rows of these cabinets, and each had garage-like fireproof doors that my fellow file clerks and I would lift at the start of the day and pull down at the end of the day. The only lighting was from overhead fluorescent bulbs, which illuminated the dingy, ink-streaked white walls of our workspace set deep in the second level of the basement. As if to emphasize the machine-like work we were doing, all the file clerks wore ugly blue-grey smocks. The job required very little thought, so I easily developed a routine that got all my work done by late afternoon; then, I could help others who were running a little slow.

My speedy work was recognized, and I was promoted to be the trainer of the file clerks, working under a woman named Susan. She was one of the new managers, and she was young and had great fashion sense. Everybody seemed to like the energy she brought to the department, and when she had an idea, everyone listened. When I first met Susan, she handed me a catalog of training classes the bank offered its employees. She told me to come back the next day and tell her what classes I wanted to attend.

I took the catalog home with me that night and examined it, and I told Susan the next morning that I didn't see anything I needed to learn. Looking back now, I can clearly see that I was so enmeshed in the routine I'd developed at work—the routine that helped me tear through my work as fast as possible—that I couldn't even see that it was going to take more for me to be successful in my new job as a trainer. Susan took the catalog out of my hand and circled about ten classes. "You're taking all of these," she said, not unkindly but with finality. Suddenly I was having flashback to Mr. MacDonald thrusting a stack of college applications across his desk at me and telling me I'd be filling them out.

Susan's insistence that I move out of my comfort zone and start learning is the reason I am a coach today; I now know that some people need the same type of accountability I did to break their safe, comfortable routines and move forward to the next stage in life. Because of Susan, I went on to become a manager, serving in that role for ten years before I left the bank. I managed small teams, external consultants, and project teams, and later was the business manager of a group made up of well over four thousand employees.

Wonderful intermediaries like Mr. MacDonald, Mrs. Espinoza, and Susan can show us roads that lead to passions and inspiration. When you find people like these, welcome them into your life.

Beliefs and Passions

"But I don't know what my passion is . . ."

I hear these words from my clients again and again. When I ask them to spend a week or two uncovering a few things they're passionate about, some will tell me they don't have time for such an endeavor. Others take it even further, telling me they don't have a passion. At first, these responses used to trouble me, but then I realized that all of us feel this way sometimes—usually because our routines have desensitized us and made us fearful.

Identifying your passion is about finding out where the universe and you intersect. It's about finding your gift, the special something you have that will make the world a better place. And once you discover or reignite your passion, you've taken an important step toward unshackling yourself from the mindless routines that can choke the joy and success out of your life.

I do realize that taking an hour to examine your life can be scary and stressful work. What if you discover that you've ignored your passion for four decades and you are devastated by the waste? Or you discover that following your passion will mean you have to quit the job that keeps your lights on and puts bread on the table? Our desire to avoid these negative feelings in the short term can cause us to put off our passions for the familiarity of routines. But as you know, this will only lead to more frustration and heartbreak down the road. The wonderful thing is that our passions are resilient, and they keep on showing up in our lives even when we don't realize it. Even if you've been neglecting yours for years, you'll find that they haven't grown brittle and rusty.

When I had my first coaching call with Ana, she had just made one of the biggest jumps of her life. She'd worked for a massive corporation for twenty years, when suddenly the company went through a reorganization. Everything changed, and not to Ana's liking. She explained to me that she'd decided to leave on her own terms, even though giving up the comfort of her work routine had been extremely difficult. Now she was in a new exploratory stage of her life. Despite her decision, I could hear in her voice a sense of disappointment over the reality of being forced into making this choice.

In a series of phone calls, Ana and I did several deep dives into her past, her fundamental beliefs about life, and the things she'd felt passionate about over the years. "I always felt best when I was helping someone else," she told me, and it kept coming back to that. At work, she'd relished every opportunity to counsel her colleagues and had even taken classes to get some counseling credentials.

"I want you to think about this passion for giving aid and counsel to others, and what your life would look like if you decided to follow that passion wherever it took you," I told Ana. She promised she would. On our next call, there was a gushing energy in her voice I hadn't heard before.

"I'm going to do this!" Ana said. "I'm going to do what it takes to follow this through." Sure enough, over the following months, Ana built herself a new career around her passion for counseling. When I followed up with her several months later, she had a growing roster of clients, but more importantly, she was suffused with joy. She'd broken out of her decades-long work routine in a moment of crisis, but following her passion had kept her from slipping back into a rut. She was building herself a new and better reality.

I've seen this happen again and again with my clients—a longstanding routine is shed for good based on the person's willingness to jump into the deep end of their passions in life.

Effective Goal Setting

A firm belief or a burning passion can do a lot to propel us out of our limiting routines, but if we want to sustain our forward momentum, we have to learn how to set—and achieve—goals. However, the comfortable, mindless routines of daily life tend to hover in the background, preventing us from achieving those goals. Thus, we must make the effort to build a plan for ourselves and take the actions that lead us toward personal fulfillment.

Most of us first become familiar with goal setting in the workplace. Maybe you sit down with your manager every quarter and set performance benchmarks for the upcoming period. Maybe you strive to meet a certain level of productivity—producing a certain amount of widgets in a certain amount of time—in the hope that this will lead to recognition, or even a promotion. Maybe you even use "SMART" goals—those that are Specific, Measurable, Attainable, Realistic, and Time Bound. In recent decades, the American workplace seems to be caught up in a goal-setting mania.

Certainly, working toward goals on the job can be positive, but it needs to be expanded beyond the workplace and into our personal lives if we want to reap the full benefits of goal setting. When the economy crashed in 2008 and fifteen million people found themselves suddenly without jobs, many of us learned the hard way that life consists of much more than our jobs. We must remember that our jobs are a means to an end, not the other way around.

So, what are your dreams for your personal life? Where are the goals that encompass the person you are outside of work? Over the course of this book, we'll examine what you want your life to look like in five years (the Life Plan) and explore how you can make definitive progress toward achieving them.

When we have clear goals that align with our beliefs and passions, we no longer feel lost or plan-less. We feel that our efforts have a purpose, and we no longer feel like we must fall back on the mind-numbing, limiting routines that can all too easily overgrow our lives. No matter how old you are and no matter what's happened in your life, you still have time to get back on the path to your Life Plan.

Let's get started by laying some groundwork for the Life Plan in the following exercise.

Exercise 1.1: Create Your Timeline

Now that we've examined how routines can limit our lives, I want to take you to a deeper, more personal look at your own life. They say a picture is worth a thousand words, so we're going to create a visual representation—a timeline—of your life so far. It will be like looking through a crystal ball, only we're looking not at your future (that will come soon enough) but at your past.

This timeline exercise is designed to help you see your life in linear stages and scrutinize each one. It will help you look for where certain behaviors and routines that may be running your life originated, and it will help you pinpoint emerging passions—and hopefully reveal the routines you either broke or will have to break to allow them to flourish.

When I first did this exercise, I had several epiphanies about myself. My timeline showed me that I had been teaching others since high school, when I first volunteered to help a first-grade class learn to read. I then saw that in every job I had, I was always teaching others how to do their jobs more effectively and efficiently. In retrospect, my job as a trainer at the bank had been no coincidence: my timeline showed me a clear trail of training and teaching others as a passion.

I also learned that my need to volunteer was rooted in the fact that I can use my gifts and my experiences to make the world a better place. I saw evidence of helping others all through my timeline, from volunteering to help the school with a program to lessen the dropout rate at my high school, to teaching children how to read, to putting on events for some of the many clubs I was involved in at the school.

I also saw a routine that had driven my life ever since the day my mother surprised me by dropping me off at kindergarten. From that day forward, even at five years old, I told myself I would never be caught off guard again. I began developing routines, some of which still show up in my life today, to protect me from ever having to feel that scared again. One of these routines is my habit of always having to know what's next. For example, I am extremely organized. In fact, many who know me, when asked to describe me with one word, would say *organized*. This might at first seem like a strength, but I know that it can also be crippling: being organized applies not only to physical space but to our mental state as well. For years, I wouldn't contribute in meetings at work because I felt the need to organize my thoughts before I spoke. By the time I was done organizing, someone else had beat me to the punch. This became a big professional obstacle, since a reluctance to participate is often viewed as weakness or disinterest. I was often told to be more assertive, or even aggressive. But I didn't realize what a big problem it was until my boss's boss called me into her office one day and blasted me for not saying a word in a meeting.

"Why are you even there?" she asked curtly. "You never say a word." Years later, the timeline gave me insight into how that feeling of always needing to be organized and on top of things had brought me to an impasse in my career.

As I scanned the first timeline I ever made and took a broad view of my life, I could see certain years when routines were driving my life, and thus no growth or major accomplishments surfaced. But then there were years in which change did occur—sometimes good and sometimes bad—and it was always because I'd broken a limiting routine. This exercise helped me understand that who I am today is the product of my past, my present, and my future. I hope that you'll have a similar revelation as you build your own timeline.

One word of caution before you begin this exercise: it may provoke emotions you have suppressed for years. I've had a couple of clients who remembered painful sexual abuse in their early years and realized that their failure to deal with that pain had arrested their adult lives. If something like that happens to you, please seek professional counseling as you work through that area of your life.

This is one of the most powerful exercises I have ever done. It alone can change a person's life, as I've seen in several of my clients. Even when the truth the timeline reveals is a hard one, the effect can be positive. One of my clients—one of those who discovered abuse in her past—discovered that the early abuse had likely influenced her poor choice in spouses: she'd suffered through a marriage to an abusive husband for over a decade. Realizing that this pattern of victimhood had begun in childhood was a huge breakthrough for her. It helped her realize why she'd been attracted to someone like her ex-husband and served as the starting point for the routine-breaking journey she had ahead of her.

If you take the time and really dig deep into your past, you will better understand who you are today. The timeline will reveal to you whether the routines you have created in the past—and the beliefs behind them—are still active and controlling your life today. It should also reveal your core passions in life, the things that nourish you and that you love to do. In the next chapter, we'll explore these passions more deeply as we take our next step toward completing your Life Plan.

But for now, take a large blank sheet of paper and turn it to a landscape orientation. Draw a long line in the center of the page, from the left margin to the right margin.

Next, write "1" as the far left side of the line, and your current age at the right side. Segment the line into five pieces; each one will represent one fifth of your life so far. Write the approximate ages at each of the four points between "1" and your current age, as shown here.

For each fifth, think about what stands out for you during that particular time in your life. Record what you remember about that time in your life; the major events that occurred. Write small or on a diagonal (or make your timeline big) so you can fit all your major memories in each interval. Try using different colors to indicate major milestones. If you're feeling creative, you can use stickers and other crafts.

I also want you to write down the names of the influential people and mentors in your life, adding them to the segment of your life where they had the biggest impact.

When you're done, the timeline should reflect most of the major events and people in your life.

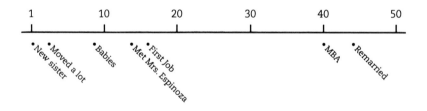

Examine the timeline for trends across the different intervals. This could take minutes, but you might want to take a couple of days to ponder the timeline. When you're ready, ask yourself the following questions:

1. Looking closely at the first ten years of your life, did certain events shape your beliefs about the world?
2. Did you create routines or safety mechanisms in your life based on an early event that was uncomfortable or traumatic, or that created a certain belief in you?
3. Do you see times of retreat from the world? What was going on when you drew back?
4. What mentors show up in your timeline? How do you think they influenced the progression of your life?
5. How does your passion show up across the timeline? Do you see early signs of it? Has it continued to show up consistently, or has it become conspicuously absent?
6. Do you see times of amazing growth? What triggered the growth?
7. Do you see years of focus? If yes, what was the focus and what did it render? Did you effectively set and achieve any major life goals?
8. Do you see routines? Can you see how they helped or stifled your path?

Chapter 2

What Do You Really Control?

▶▶ I know you've heard that we all get twenty-four hours in a day. And it's true: whether you're the president of the United States, the CEO of a company, a stay-at-home mom, or an assistant in an office, position does not grant you an extra minute. We are all bound by the forward momentum of minutes, hours, days, months, and years. Time is given to each of us in the same amount. And, much to the delight of the plastic surgeons of the world, we haven't yet found a way to stop the aging of our bodies. A pull, tuck, and cut may help stave off the appearance of age for a while, but internally, we're all moving forward at precisely the same rate.

The unstoppable progression of time tends to make us uncomfortable. No matter how much we'd like to, none of us can control the passing of time. And time is just one example of the things we humans can't control. What about the economy? Our lives might have been going quite well back in 2007, but how did many of us feel when the 2008 financial crisis threatened our futures? Suddenly, the news of financial giants beginning to fail: Goldman Sachs, Merrill Lynch, and Lehman Brothers all rocked our world. The impact of the financial collapse—and its ongoing global impact—made many people feel powerless.

In the natural world, we face different types of calamities

that can turn our lives upside down. Think about Hurricanes Katrina, Rita, and George—all of which caused devastating damage in the Caribbean and along the Gulf Coast. The people who were impacted by these terrible storms may have been doing everything right, and may have been following their dream, but then—BAM! A force beyond their control changed life forever.

Clearly, there are plenty of things in our lives that we have absolutely no control over. We must understand that despite our best efforts to live our lives the way we want to, external circumstances dictate much of what happens to us.

But is that an excuse for giving up on the parts of our lives we *do* control? The argument of this book is a resounding "NO." Quite the opposite: the fact that we don't control everything should encourage us to focus more intently on the things we can control. If you want to live the life you dream of and achieve the goals you aspire toward, it's imperative that you ignore the things you can't control and home in on the things you can. It's the same wise advice we know from the popular Serenity Prayer: "God, grant me the serenity to accept the things I cannot change, courage to change the things I can, and wisdom to know the difference."

Seize Control, or Control Seizes You

"Hey Luz, your anniversary's coming up soon, right?" my co-worker chirped.

I smiled politely and answered in the affirmative but quickly moved on. What I wanted to say was, "Please, please, *don't* remind me."

I'd started working at the bank at age twenty, and I had a significant milestone coming up soon: twenty-five years at the company. The bank published a list of employees who had reached the quarter-century mark, and though it had the best of intentions, seeing my name on that list was something I'd been dreading for months. It would mean that I was old. Washed up. Stuck.

The prospect of making that list had triggered an epiphany in me at the age of forty-four. I was leading a life I hadn't chosen. I was skimming along, tied down in a web of routines and controlled by all the forces both large and small. The one force missing was my own power to control my destiny. I knew it was time to leave my comfort zone at the bank.

But how on earth can you do that, Luz? said a voice in my head. *You've got two kids in college and a thirteen-year-old at home. And you're the head of the household!*

If I could've looked forward twenty-five years from the age of twenty, this certainly wasn't the life I would've pictured—or desired. At that time, I was studying to be a bilingual teacher. I'd been inspired by Mrs. Espinoza, and I knew the success of many young Latina girls in Chicago was going to depend on having a strong role model—a capable woman who came from a similar background who was making it in the world. I wanted to be that person for them. I wanted to pay it forward and pass on the mentoring I'd received by graduating college and then teaching in a Chicago public school with a dense Latino population. That was my dream. And I wanted to see the world, too—second up in job choices would've been one that allowed me to travel. I pictured myself as a flight attendant soaring around the globe or as a renowned archaeologist on a dig in Egypt. Maybe that last one was a little far-fetched, but being a bilingual teacher in the Chicago public school system, with a little volunteering on the side, sounds like a simple, achievable dream, right?

Of course, that's not how it happened. Thanks to my epiphany regarding my job at the bank, I realized that I'd been living a life I didn't choose. My twenty-year-old self never would've set a course for single-motherhood, a wearying job, and fifty-hour workweeks. But my life had been unplanned; it had been dictated by others. I wasn't controlling; I was being controlled.

I'd gotten married at the tender age of twenty-one just a week after I turned twenty-one. Marriage was the last thing on my mind when I met the handsome, popular guy I would end up marrying. My mind was still full of dreams for my life. But the wedding just happened, and at first, our life together seemed great.

Likewise, when I'd accepted the job at the bank shortly before my marriage, it had started out fine. It was predictable and stable. I knew what time to arrive, how to do my work, and when I could go home. I added another layer of routine when I went back to school part-time: I knew what bus to get on, which classes to take, what books to study. Then came the kids, along with a fresh layer: more bus schedules; more activities; more predictable, recurring events. I had to run a tight ship to keep all these routines going. My life was scheduled down to the minute, and there was no time for reading *Cosmo* or romance novels, seeing a movie with my girlfriends, or spending any time on my own, and I certainly wasn't making time to think about where this regimented, packed-to-the-gills existence was taking me.

The routines ratcheted up a notch once I got divorced. I'd ignored some early instances of infidelity, but when the same old story repeated itself again, we had a breakup that finally stuck. I was left alone to care for three beautiful children—one eight years old, one four years old, and the third just nine months old.

Years later, I was facing the prospect of the twenty-five-year list at the bank, and it had hit me like a ton of bricks that I wasn't happy. Certainly there were things I wouldn't have changed—my kids and my education, for example—but I knew that if I'd designed my life, this wasn't what it would've looked like.

A crucial part of this epiphany was the fact that I'd recently learned about the concept of intentionality and how it could help me build the life I really wanted. Thanks to a lucky series of events, I realized that living with intention was the only way to take control of my life and to start steering it toward the destination I hoped to arrive at one day. After I completed my MBA at the University of Chicago, I got a big promotion to a position that sounded perfect to me. My boss at the time, who still ranks as one of the best I've had in my career, asked me to take part in a "transformational coaching" program for about sixty executives. The program was based on some core competencies in the coaching world, and it included exercises that helped participants examine their lives from the past, the present, and the future. It was a six-month program, and it required us to meet for eight hours one or two days a month.

In these sessions, I learned about life declarations and life direction as a tool to lead me to the path of the life I had been dreaming about, but it required the shattering of those routines and beliefs in my life that were holding me back from achieving my life's dream. I must admit, I was skeptical about the whole thing at first, since I am a person driven by facts and logic, and some of the principles of this approach felt a little wishful and vague. And I struggled with it as a person of faith, too. I felt like some of the things we were learning were bordering on God's territory—one young executive in the program had piped up to make a comment on using positive thinking to obliterate AIDS from the world. A worthy cause, I thought, but maybe too big of a stretch.

Nevertheless, I decided to try this intentional way of living. Intentionality meant that before I encountered a situation, I needed to set an intention so that I could be in control of the situation.

Here's a simple personal example: At the time, I was dealing with an employee who challenged everyone, including me. He was an older man, and he didn't like the fact that he was now working for a woman a lot younger than he was. He was very skilled in his profession, but he lacked interpersonal skills, and there had been several complaints about the way he treated other people, women in particular. I knew firsthand how he was, having been the target of his dismissive, patronizing attitude several times. One day, as I was headed into a meeting with this individual, I decided to not let him control the meeting—as would've been typical of me before—and instead set the intention of maintaining my power, speaking my mind, and not getting upset with him no matter what he said. I did just that. After I met a few of his mildly belittling comments with determination and strength, he backed down. He listened. He grew quieter. Lo and behold, setting an intention beforehand and sticking with it had worked!

After that experience, I found myself wondering how different my life would've been if I'd taken this tool and applied it broadly to my life as twenty-year-old college girl. *Why didn't someone tell me to create a plan for my life?* I thought. *I could've written down exactly what I wanted and then gone straight after it. Things would be so different now!*

As it turns out, it would take me a few more years to successfully implement intentionality in my own life. Just after my twenty-fifth anniversary on the job, the bank merged with another bank, and my bosses didn't want to let me go. I asked for a package that would let me out; instead, I got a promotion and more money. As often happens, something that at first appears positive had become a barrier and was making it more difficult to reach the life I wanted. Then, finally, after twenty-eight years of service, I accepted a new job offer. I was out, but I'd spent a whole lot of years living a professional life I never really chose.

Does my experience sound familiar to you? Have you been where I was at some point in your life? Are you there now? Many of my clients come to me for coaching because they are suddenly struck by that terrible feeling I had—that I was wasting time in a life that was entirely controlled by other people and other forces. They find themselves saying things like "I'll do it someday" or "Eventually I'll have the time to do that." But they're so stuck in their routines, and they feel so buffeted by events and circumstances they can't control that they always end up running back to the comfort of a job that seems "okay" and the mind-numbing habits that keep them busy.

Let me take you back for a second to illustrate my point. Think back to those years when you felt like you had your whole life in front of you, when you were between eighteen to twenty-two years old. Some of you were experiencing the routine of college and working toward a career. If you were fortunate, you were not footing the college bill and had your parent's home as a security blanket. You probably never had a concern about where your next meal would come from (despite probably saying, "I'm starving" all the time). In other words, since life was good, there was never a need to create a plan or to be intentional with how you were going to live. But let's suppose for a moment that you *had* taken some time to write a Life Plan. What would it have contained?

Don't write anything down now, but think about what your dreams for your life would have been like if you had written them down when you were eighteen years old. (It might be scary and very different from what you want now—and that's okay!)

In the next chapter, we're going to explore how the Life Plan can help us overcome the labels other people place on us (and that we place on ourselves), and then, in the chapters that follow, we'll start constructing your current Life Plan.

Chapter 3

Overcoming Labels

▶ ▶ I'll never forget Angelo, a redheaded boy in my fourth-grade class—not because he was a friend but because of what he said to me one day on the playground during recess.

"From far away you look pretty, but up close you're ugly," Angelo told me.

It was one of the many stupid, cruel things I heard uttered during my grade-school years, but the day Angelo spat that at me, I stood horrified, my heart in my stomach. *Has everyone noticed this about me?* my ten-year-old mind wondered.

You can't imagine how deeply that one moment in my life scarred me. For years, I believed that people would see me from afar and think that I was attractive but then change their minds as soon as they got up close and personal. It stuck with me well into high school, and I even started dating unattractive guys, thinking I had no chance of doing any better, what with a face that didn't stand up to close scrutiny.

But finally, I started to see evidence that the insecurity Angelo had saddled me with wasn't based in reality. "You're so pretty," my best friend's dad told me one day. "I bet you have the pick of all the boys at school." A few days later, I was standing behind the register of a McDonald's—my glamorous after-school job—when a man walked up and asked whether I was

Luz. When I told him yes, he said, "I thought so. I'm a friend of your dad's, and he told me you'd be the prettiest one here." Bit by bit, I started to build confidence in my appearance. And yet Angelo's comment haunted me even in adulthood. Though the man I married was quite good-looking, I still found myself wondering if I was pretty enough for him.

I tell you this story because it's a perfect example of something that holds many of us back from living full, fulfilling lives: the labels that others give us. No matter what your background is, I'm certain you've been given a few. Maybe you were told at a young age that you would be this or that—very smart, a dreamer, a go-getter. Or maybe you heard more negative descriptions of yourself: perhaps you were told you were lazy, unrealistic, or indecisive, or you were given some other descriptor you still remember. These labels tend to shape our lives, especially at a very young age, just as Angelo's remark shaped my self-image in a powerful and lasting way.

In school, we see more labels thrown upon us; most of the time they are unspoken. Yet, it becomes evident when the teacher calls on the same students for answers in the classroom that some students have a power that the rest of us do not have or even understand. We begin to tell ourselves that we are not smart enough, and we eventually begin to believe it.

It gets worse when we enter the working world. We meet so many people that we throw labels on them based on a few interactions or based on what we've heard—and the same is done to us. And those awful quarterly performance reviews begin to tell us the many ways we can improve; the list of weaknesses we need to fix never seems to end. And, as if that isn't enough, many of us get 360° peer reviews, which—though they can be helpful—can also reinforce the negative labels we feel are applied to us. In my mind, the entire performance evaluation process can feel like being thrown in a ring with Muhammad Ali, getting pummeled for the first three rounds, then being finished off by Joe Frazier and Rocky Balboa. Then, after this beating, you're expected to go back to your desk and find a way to be better just to keep your job. Too often, we come out on the other end of a supposedly "constructive" review with a newly reinforced negativity about ourselves.

I know firsthand how tough it is not to be affected by other people's conception of you, especially at work. Years ago, I transferred departments within my company to begin doing work as a project manager. No more than six weeks into the job, my manager called me into her office. There she sat with one of my fellow project managers. I wasn't immediately alarmed, as I'd noticed some clear politicking going on in the department, with plenty of closed-door meetings to which I wasn't invited. Sure enough, their message wasn't pleasant. In essence, it was "You don't know how to do your job as a project manager."

At that point, I had two clear choices: I could either believe that I was indeed a bad project manager like they were telling me, or I could ignore what they were saying based on my ten years of successful project management. At that point in my career, I was confident enough to reject the label they were trying to stick on me, but imagine if I'd accepted it. A decade of experience would've added up to uselessness! After I told my boss and this fellow project manager that I disagreed with their assessment, they took me off the project, and my colleague actually got my office. Nevertheless, I'd made the right decision. I moved to another project and soon became a respected team lead. Six months after the move, the project manager who'd criticized me apologized to me, saying she'd "misjudged my value." She had misjudged me, but I was just grateful I didn't buy in to her assessment!

We Were Made for So Much More

The absurdity of letting labels rule our lives becomes so strikingly apparent when we think about what incredible creatures each of us is. From a purely scientific point of view, we are indeed a marvel. The list of wonders is endless, but one of my favorites is the fact that, if stretched out into a line, one person's DNA molecules would cover several cities in length. And have you ever thought about the marvels of the human eye? There are so many layers, with each performing a different role—the expanding and contracting pupil, the refracting cornea, the adjusting lens, and the highly sensitive retina, not to mention our eyelids and tears, which keep out foreign objects and keep our eyes clear. The brain, too, is an almost unfathomably incredible organ, dwarfing the achievements of even our most advanced computers. How could a being who possesses such incredible powers subject himself or herself to harmful labels?

Even more incredible than the capabilities of our bodies, though, is the power of the human spirit. If we tap into that power, we can overcome any label placed on us, no matter how damaging. Dr. Samuel Betances, a sociologist, is a wonderful example. I had the pleasure of hearing Dr. Betances speak to a group of high school students one Saturday morning—I was in the audience supporting a nonprofit organization. This man captivated the audience, making us howl in laughter and then telling gripping stories that moved many of us to tears. At one point in his talk, he told us that he dropped out of high school primarily because, due to his low attendance rate, the school had labeled him a "bad" kid who had no future. For years after dropping out, he lived his life under that label, until he met an older woman who challenged him to move beyond it. This woman told the young Samuel Betances that he needed to read the stories of other people who lived through adversity and that biographies, autobiographies, and memoirs were a great way to do that.

At first, Samuel balked. "I don't have the time for all that reading!" he told her. The woman wasn't about to take such a lame excuse. She found two hours in his schedule for the next week and held him accountable to reading. With that, Samuel was off, devouring inspirational real-life stories like candy. Particularly influential for him were those of great orators like Martin Luther King, Jr., and several U.S. presidents, and he soon found that he, too, could project his voice and move and persuade with his words. In doing so, he was dismissing that "bad kid" label that had been inflicted upon him. In essence, he had learned to reject rejection. Given that breakthrough, it's no surprise that he went on to obtain a master's and a doctorate from Harvard.

Patrick Henry Hughes, too, overcame a label—in his case, that of "the blind boy." Because he was born without eyes, many assumed his future would be dark and that the value he offered to society would be small. Yet Patrick's parents never allowed anyone to label him as someone on the margin. Instead, they nurtured the incredible talent he showed for music from the time he was a toddler. Years later, he was asked to join a university marching band. Patrick's parents didn't quite believe it at first, but they reasoned that if the band director wanted Patrick to do it, they would be behind him 100 percent. Patrick and his father ended up not only playing in the band but also marching with them; Patrick plays trumpet from his wheelchair. "God made me blind and crippled," he says, "but he also gave me the ability to play music and meet people, and so that is what I am going to do." Last time I checked, a YouTube video that tells Patrick's story had 2.7 million views.

Despite examples like these and despite everything that is wonderful and awe-inspiring about us, we are still deeply vulnerable to other people's opinions of us. But the danger, as we've seen, lies in the fact that other people's opinions of us are not always true. To withstand criticism and labeling, you must know yourself, because you will encounter many negative people in your lifetime that will try to tell you who you are. But they are wrong. Dead wrong. Their motives are bad, and you must be able to dismiss these people quickly and forge ahead being who you are to achieve your Life Plan.

But here's another important consideration: don't put yourself on a pedestal and think that only others do this—examine yourself to see whether you, too, are guilty of labeling and judging the people around you. I have done this more than I care to confess. I once attended a presentation where I was immediately put off by the speaker. As soon as this woman walked across the stage, I saw that she was impeccably dressed and looked like her life was perfect. *I don't want to hear what* she *has to say*, I said to myself. Well, once she told her story—which involved the fact that her only son had shot and killed a man—I quickly realized that my judgment of her was completely off. Honestly, I felt horrible for my inaccurate snap judgment. I'm sure you can think of similar situations in your own life. But as we do our best to escape the labels others place on us, we should make sure that we're not causing the same kind of harm to people around us.

Your Life Plan Will Help You Overcome Labels

As you create your Life Plan in the remaining chapters of this book, you'll find that you're equipping yourself with the tools necessary to know yourself, see your own worth, and not succumb to other people's judgments of you. When I look at my Life Plan, I get a clear picture of who I am today and where I am going. Since I created it, it contains no judgments from others. With it, I am not trying to please anyone but myself. It takes a great deal of honesty and courage to strip away the labels that others have inflicted on us—in my case, to see myself as beautiful versus Angelo's label of me as ugly. So when I look at my Life Plan, I see a positive picture of me. I see myself financially stable. I see myself strong and healthy. I see myself running a successful business. I see me.

I have had many clients who are stuck in jobs—and lives—they never really wanted. Every year, they receive performance reviews telling them they are doing a good job, so year after year they keep doing the same work over and over, never really challenging the labels applied to them. Just when they think that they are ready to make a change and quit the job that no longer nourishes them, something changes to convince them to stay even longer. A year turns into two, then to five, then eight, twelve, and so on. The employee buys more and more into the label "employee of such-and-such company" and begins to believe he or she is stuck for life. It happened to me, too—for years, I accepted the label of "banker," never realizing that wasn't what I was at all.

The good news is that when people start creating a Life Plan and really thinking about what they want out of life, fear falls away and they are empowered to shed their labels. When that happens, a whole new world opens up before them. It wasn't until I developed my Life Plan—which identified me as more entrepreneur than banker—that I left the bank and shed my "banker" label. But doing so ushered me into a whole new phase of life.

Exercise 3.1: Examining Your Labels

1. Think about the labels you have been given in life, and identify where they came from. Which ones still hold the most sway in your life?
2. Write down your unique value to the world. What you do you bring to the table?
3. What labels have you successfully shed over the course of your life? What did it take to drop them?
4. What labels are you giving to the people around you?

Chapter 4

What Really Matters to You?

▶▶ The ultimate purpose of breaking out of our limiting routines will be to construct a new Life Plan, one that reflects our passions and aspirations. This Life Plan will serve as a road map for moving toward a fulfilling life and will help us live with intention. But before we get started on it, we need to lay the foundation for what comes ahead. In this chapter, I want you to take some time to think about the things that matter to you.

This is a crucial step in the process of building a Life Plan. It helps you solidify who you really are, deep down—and that's important because if we build a Life Plan for the person we just think we are (or the person we just want to be) instead of who we *actually are*, the plan will do no good. Our passions in life—the people, ideas, and activities that matter to us—define us, yet they can fade away all too easily. As we discussed in chapter 1, our routines can all too easily mask or subvert the things we love. Sometimes we put up blocks against what inspires and moves us—perhaps those things embarrass us, or we don't want to pursue them because we're too scared we might fail in front of everyone.

The exercises in this chapter are designed to help you move past these routines and self-imposed restrictions and take a closer look at the things that give your life meaning, including vocations, hobbies, causes, and the people in your life. Before you move ahead in this chapter, find a quiet place and make sure you've carved out at least an hour to complete the exercises. Grab a pen and paper, or you can write in the blank pages provided in this book. (But do write. You may be tempted to wing it, and just spend a few minutes thinking about these exercises. I've seen in my experience, though, that this is not nearly as effective as taking the time and effort to actually write down your thoughts and feelings.)

One more thing: let's get you in a positive, peaceful head-space before we start. I want you to imagine a perfect day, the most relaxed, inviting scenario you can picture, whatever that looks like for you. Here's an example: The sun is shining brightly. It's still early morning, and the temperature is hovering at about seventy-five degrees. You're sitting outside, and about three hundred feet in front of you is a beautiful, calm lake glistening in the sunlight. Birds are singing a beautiful melody all around you, butterflies are zooming by, and the soft wind carries a sweet smell from the flowers nearby. Take in the aroma, close your eyes, and listen to the music of nature. Take a deep breath. Feel a complete sense of calmness in your soul. Feel the cool breeze. Breathe it in one more time.

You're now ready to begin exercise 4.1.

Exercise 4.1: Things I Love

Start this exercise by thinking about the things you love in life. Don't let anyone else's opinions or any pressures you feel— from friends, coworkers, family, or society—interfere with your brainstorm. For example, one of my clients struggled with the difference between loving her mother and siblings and loving the forty-minute drive to spend every Sunday with her mother and siblings. She felt like she *should* love making these trips every time, but if she was honest with herself, they were eating up precious time. She eventually got to a place where she could say that she loved her family but didn't have to act like she enjoyed the expectation that she'd visit every single Sunday. As the things you love start to occur to you and you begin to write them down, look for similar distinctions. Don't write down that you love something just because your mom or your boss or your husband or anyone else would expect you to or just because you feel like you should.

In your list of things you love, include items from all aspects of your life, whether they're personal or professional. In the other exercises in this chapter, you're going to focus more closely on the people and causes you hold dear, but don't let that prevent you from writing anything that might fall in those categories here.

Consider these questions to help keep the ideas flowing freely from your pen: What are the things you would do if you were not tethered to the routines you have mastered since grammar school? What if you controlled the hands of the clock—what would you do with that time? Who are the people you would spend time with? What types of books would you read? What outdoor activities would you enjoy or try out for the first time?

Here's an example of what the first few items on your list might look like:

- I love spring, when everything comes back to life.
- I love a day without back-to-back meetings.
- I loved the pottery class I took ten years ago.
- I love spending time in my local library.
- I love snowshoeing after a fresh snowfall.

▸ I love to sit in the local coffee house with my husband while we have an amazing cup of coffee and an indescribably delicious chocolate donut.

Are you getting plenty of ideas down? Are you feeling the passion and satisfaction these things bring you?

If you free up your mind and allow yourself to participate in this exercise fully, your list is going to be long. Dig deep, and make the list as lengthy as it needs to be.

When you're done, look back over the list. Read each item to yourself, and judge whether it makes you feel any kind of stress or anxiety. If it does, cross it off right away. You want this list to be populated with things that make you smile as you visualize doing them. If you feel stress when thinking about something you wrote down, it's likely that the love you feel for it is not emanating from inside but is instead the product of some external pressure.

Exercise 4.2: Things I Hate

The "Things I Love" exercise you just did let you get lost in the things in life that make you passionate and happy—and now you're probably feeling pretty good. I don't want to ruin the moment, but I'm afraid I have to temporarily. So that you fully understand your loves and passions, we must also look at the flipside: the things that stress you out and annoy you, the things you hate.

When we really hate something, it's easy to tell because usually our bodies give off immediate signals of distress when we have to do them. I used to absolutely *hate* when I was forced to attend meetings if I really didn't have anything to contribute or there wasn't anything I could learn from them.

But it seemed to happen often—because of the mere fact that I was part of certain project teams, I'd constantly be invited to meetings. Every time, I would immediately ask why I had to attend, and when the responses were not in my favor, I would begin to get angry. I would then begin to complain to anyone who'd listen about how ineffective and inefficient these meetings were. Before I knew it, my anger and frustration over a single meeting had hijacked my mind and body, and I'd remain in its control for days.

As you make your own list of things you hate, think about the situations that provoke a similar reaction in you. These are the banes of your existence, the things you dread, the things that prevent you from doing what you love, and the things that occupy your mind far longer than they have any right to. Here are a few more of mine:

- I hate days of back-to-back meetings.
- I hate being around negative people.
- I hate winter.
- I hate early morning meetings (I'm definitely not a morning person).
- I hate being in lines—in traffic, at store checkouts, at crowded events, etc.
- I hate being unorganized.

Once you've gotten your first burst out, examine your list. Is anything missing? As you look back over what you've written, a few more will probably occur to you. Jot those down, too.

Now read the entire list again. You may feel disappointment and frustration, especially as you realize that several of these things are occupying quite a bit of space in your life. Breathe deeply and relax as you try to let those negative feelings go. Soon, you'll be taking action to eliminate some of these hated things from your life and ensure that the ones you can't get rid of aren't holding you back from the life you deserve.

Exercise 4.3: People Who Matter to Me

I hope you're feeling some relief at getting all that negativity on paper and out of your head for the time being. Now we're going to move back to things that love and inspire you, this time with a focus on the people in your life who really matter to you.

Children, Spouses, Significant Others

If you're a parent, it's a safe bet that your kids are going to be at the top of the list. If your children are still young, your life revolves around them, but no matter how old they are, your sons or daughters are the people who likely bring the greatest richness to your existence. If you're a parent, start by writing your child's name (or children's names) at the top of your "People Who Matter to Me" list.

If you have a spouse or significant other, that person will probably be right under your kids on this list. If so, write that person's name down too. But this Life Plan groundwork we're doing is no place for lying: if your marriage is failing or if you're trapped in a negative relationship or your bond with your child is "broken" at the moment, you're not obligated to list that person here. Maybe your thoughts on that matter are best suited for the "Things I Hate" list—as in, "I hate how I feel when my husband . . ." or "I hate the frustration I feel around my girlfriend when . . ."

If you're single and not a parent, you can set up this domain to cover the handful of people you're closest to in life, no matter who they are. The idea is to create a special focus for the people who are most important to us—to distinguish them from the much wider and ever-changing circle of friends and coworkers and acquaintances around us.

Extended Family, Friends, and Coworkers

Next, I want you to think about all the other people in your family who really matter to you—parents, siblings, aunts, uncles, cousins, stepparents, and so on.

Then go a step further and think about your closest friends, the coworkers you have a strong relationship with, your mentors, your neighbors, and anyone else in your life who matters to you. Write down the names from these various clusters of people who hold a special place in your life. After I listed my family, the "friends" portion of my list started with the four women I'm closest to: Mary, Sandy, Ling, and Farida, who also served as my bridesmaids.

When I say that I want you to list the people who "matter to you," I'm referring to the people with whom you want to have a relationship over the next five to ten years. Several years ago, on New Year's Eve, my date and I decided to go to a New Year's Eve party—there would be a five-course meal along with music provided by a live band. We'd be going by ourselves, though, since it was a last-minute decision and many of our friends and family couldn't join us. When we arrived, there were hats and noisemakers on every table and balloons were suspended above, ready to be dropped at midnight. The room buzzed with excitement for the New Year.

A host quickly seated us at a table for the evening celebration, and at first glance, our placement seemed to be a bit of a mismatch: they were all sixty-five years old and over, while I was about thirty-two and my date just a few years older.

I decided, however, that we were going to have a good time no matter what. The night of festivities had just begun, and I was wearing a beautiful evening gown! As the night went on, we all got to know each other, and I learned that the group of about eight older people at the table had been friends for years. They were here to ring in another year together, just as they had many times before.

The more we talked, the more I was struck by the bonds between them. They told me that they had been involved in all the important parts of each other's lives—births, anniversaries, career milestones, and even deaths of loved ones. These friends clearly meant a lot to each other. Their interactions were affectionate, joyful, relaxed. It made me very aware of the fact that I longed to have friendships like these in my life. It also brought to light the fact that this guy I was with—and whom I'd been dating for years—was probably not the one for me. When my date left for the men's room at one point, one of the women leaned toward me and conspiratorially encouraged me to make sure I was spending time with people who really cared about me; from her tone, I knew she was talking about my date. Earlier in the night, the whole table had seemed surprised when they found out that I'd been dating him for nearly four years and he still hadn't proposed.

The time I spent with that group of close-knit friends on New Year's Eve really shook me. I knew I wanted what they had: a set of friends with whom I had a true bond. I determined then and there that in order to have those types of friends in my life, I needed to be deliberate in selecting those friendships, and in maintaining them. As you're writing your "People Who Matter to Me" list and reviewing it once you're done, remember that you're listing those individuals you'd want to be at your figurative New Year's Eve table.

Be mindful that real relationships are difficult to maintain, so you'll want to pare your list back to a maximum of ten people, though you may have as few as three. Strong relationships require constant contact: birthdays, weddings, funerals, barbecues, graduations, births, and social events. You'll drive yourself crazy and hurt others' feelings if you commit to too many of these, so consider your list carefully. If you've listed a coworker on the "People Who Matter to Me" list, ask yourself whether she's really a friend. Do you want to be close with her in ten years? What about your mom's friend you wrote down on your first pass? What about the guy you met at that networking event? What about the lady who added you on Facebook after meeting you once?

Narrowing your list can be difficult, but you should end up with a handful of people who matter deeply to you. Over the past ten years, my list has grown increasingly focused. Besides my family, it now consists of only six women. I make it a point to connect with these six women often, and because they are the ones who matter to me the most, when they need something from me, I am there for them, no matter what.

Exercise 4.4: Causes That Matter to Me

As I shared with you in chapter 1, my own timeline revealed that volunteering has always been a passion in my life. But even if you didn't see the same in your timeline, there are undoubtedly certain causes that are important to you. When we are connected to our communities, when we are supporting the principles and movements we feel strongly about, we are happier people who lead richer, more meaningful lives.

For that reason, I'd like you to explore the causes that matter to you before we move on to creating your Life Plan and talking about how you can start living intentionally. In what ways do you give back to your community now? What causes would you support if you had the time and/or energy? Make a list of these causes as you did in the previous exercises.

I know firsthand how supporting a cause you care about can bring fulfillment and personal growth. Having been a single mother for about eleven years, I have an affinity for helping other single mothers. I know how hard it is to be a working single mother; I completed my undergraduate and graduate degrees as I raised my children, dealing with hormone-crazed teenagers and surviving it all with several badges of honor: my oldest daughter soon will complete her PhD, my only son is pursuing his MBA, and my youngest daughter—who once hated school—is now a grammar-school teacher.

Because I know how exhausting and lonely single parenting can be, I tried to give back and support single mothers who were facing the situation I'd been through. After eleven years on my own, I married my current husband, Don—himself a father of two young boys—and he has been right by my side in these efforts. For three years, my husband and I raced out of our house every Friday night, with my two stepchildren in tow, to lead classes for the children of the single mothers at our church. We had the children, who ranged in age from ten to thirteen, every Friday night for about three hours. At first, the evening was taxing on us, since the children themselves were tired after a whole week of school, and now their single moms forced most of them to come to our class while they were in a single-mothers class. However, as we got to know the students and heard their stories, our hearts opened up and service to them became much easier.

One little boy named Adam, an only child, really touched us. He appeared to be a shy boy, since he sat alone most of the night and didn't say much. But within a few short weeks, Adam began to speak up and play the games we introduced to the children. I could tell that Adam didn't have many male figures in his life—he latched on to my husband, eager for attention and care. He and the other boys seemed to love the gym time most; that was when my husband played basketball with them. It made us realize that our time with Adam and the others was likely the only time they were with a "couple," and that was different for them. Most of the children were shuttled back and forth between their mothers' and fathers' homes, constantly rotating between two different parenting styles and two sets of rules, interrupted schedules with friends, and so on. Many were latchkey kids, just as mine were, coming home every day to a parentless house for hours.

We found that there was something quite magical that happened to these kids when they were in a room with a husband and a wife. Both my husband and I could completely relate to their lives, since we had both been divorced and our children had lived lives similar to theirs. I know that these children got a lot out of our time with them, and we benefited, too; teaching these classes helped our newly blended family start to gel into a unit. We thought we were volunteering to change the children's lives; we didn't expect it would change ours.

This is often what happens when we support causes we care about: we end up getting just as much as the ostensible beneficiaries of our efforts. There are an incalculable number of causes in the world—from saving sea turtles to curing cancer—and choosing a few to support can be overwhelming. Here, as in your "People Who Matter to Me" list, you don't want to overload yourself with ideas. My advice is that you choose cautiously and deliberately, and that you align the causes you choose with your personal interests and strengths.

I interviewed a very senior executive when I was working on my MBA, and I vividly remember him telling me that he only works with hospitals and educational organizations. *How can he be so clear on that?* I thought, and asked him a question to that effect. He went on to explain how his background and his passions aligned with hospitals and educational organizations, and he felt it best to focus on those areas. It made me think about my own alignment with the causes I support, and soon I'd narrowed my volunteering focus down to two main areas that I feel strongly about: educational programs and helping women. When I am asked to serve on boards or even to donate money, I first ask myself, "Does this cause align with my focus of women and education?" If it doesn't, it's an easy no.

At this moment, you should be feeling pretty good. You'll use the lists you made in these exercises later, but for now, set your pen aside and breathe deeply. There is something therapeutic about writing down the things we love and care about in life—it's as if writing them down releases you and gives your mind an opportunity to relax. Enjoy the moment.

There is a wonderful coaching model developed by CoachInc.com, the coaching university I attended, called the "Strategizing for Success" model. The basic premise is that you begin with the "Here and Now," which is what you've just done in this chapter. You took a deep dive into your current life and your current situation. You identified some of the good things in your life in the "Things I Love," "People Who Matter to Me," and "Causes That Matter to Me" exercises, but in the "Things I Hate" exercise, you also brought to the surface some of the biggest barriers to your happiness.

We will use this current reality you've just sketched to move toward the other side of the Strategizing for Success model: the "There and Then" side. This is where you want to be—the place where you feel fulfilled and are free of limiting routines. In the next chapter, we're going to look at how you can move closer to There and Then by taking your first steps toward intentional living. You'll soon learn that although there seem to be countless facets of our lives that we can't control, there are some that we can control. To build and carry out a Life Plan, we must learn to effectively manage the things we can control while accepting that we are powerless in some areas.

Chapter 5

Your Ten Domains: Building the Life Plan

▶ ▶ You've now taken a closer look at your life by thinking intentionally about the things that matter most to you. But you wouldn't be reading this book if you didn't want to go from your current "Here and Now" to a more fulfilling "There and Then." To do that, we're going to take a deep look at where your passions and priorities are going to take you in the future. In short, we're going to get started on your Life Plan—the tool you're going to use to design the life you want to have.

A Life Plan is, in essence, a written statement of where you want to be in the future—physically, mentally, relationally, developmentally, spiritually, and financially. The Life Plan is a clear, well-thought-out articulation of your desired future and also serves as your inspiration to move you toward that future. It's like a roadmap, a blueprint, and an itinerary all rolled up into one, with the end goal being an intentionally lived life.

Imagine that you're about to leave for an important business trip. You would've put together an itinerary, right? The itinerary would contain all the details you need to pull off a smooth, productive trip—which airline you're flying; where your hotel is, how you're getting there, and when you check-in;

a list of meeting times and the objectives of each appointment you have; and information about your flight back home. You might even have pulled up a weather forecast or made a list of some places you'd like to visit for personal pleasure—a landmark, a renowned restaurant, or a famous museum. Your itinerary is your full plan for the trip. It tells you what you're going to be doing and how you're going to do it. Your Life Plan will be similar, only instead of laying out a business trip, it will serve as a sort of itinerary for the next five years of your life.

Creating the Life Plan will also feel similar to the goal setting you already do in your professional life. I'm almost certain that in your career, a supervisor or boss has given you a set of carefully written performance objectives and held you accountable to meeting them over a period of time. Perhaps some of those objectives relate to your own development. If so, congratulations! You have a great boss or work for a great company—but most of the effort you put in to meeting goals at work will be for the benefit of the organization that employs you. With the Life Plan, you'll be setting objectives and holding yourself accountable. You'll be taking the tools used by companies and applying them to your personal life, with the aim of achieving the life you've always wanted.

By thinking systematically about your plan for the next phase of your life, you give yourself a much better chance of achieving your dreams than if you were to continue the scattershot, nebulous approach you might be employing currently. Imagine the business world without this type of strategic planning. Businesses would be failing right and left, because they wouldn't know how to get where they wanted to go—or even where they wanted to go in the first place.

This section of the book is focused on helping you develop

a lifelong practice of examining your life and declaring what you want it to look like—in writing. A life unplanned is a life that is blown here and there. A person who constantly talks about "some day" or "one day" is a person sitting around waiting for a better day that may not come. I want to help you achieve the life you want to have *now*, not down the road. And remember, no one's going to plan your life for you. *You* are the only one responsible for your own personal growth. With your Life Plan completed, you'll know where you want to be, what you want to do, when you want to do it, and who you want to be with as you do it.

To help us do this in an organized manner, we're going to start by dividing your life up into ten different areas—or what I call "domains." Of course, each of our lives has hundreds, if not thousands, of different domains, but the ten that comprise your Life Plan are going to be the ten that are most important to you. You've already started thinking about what matters to you, but now you're going to choose your ten top domains and envision how you want each of them to look in five years' time.

Why five years? Well, one year isn't ambitious enough. If you plan for just one year out, your objectives are likely to be less challenging and visionary, more predictable and mundane. The two-to-four-year range presents the same problem; you'll be more shortsighted as you plan, and you'll likely be thinking primarily about things you have going on in the present—a degree you're finishing, a certification you're pursuing, a promotion you're angling for, or the child you're raising. Five years seems to be the magic number; when you're looking that far out, it feels more like a blank slate. That blankness frees you to imagine great possibilities for the future and to start designing your life without constraints.

Exercise 5.1: Find Your Ten Domains

Ready to get going? The first thing you need to do is to identify the most important domains of your life—you're going to be picking the top ten. Here are some of the most common domains people choose:

- Relationship with spouse or significant other
- Relationship with children
- Relationship with extended family (your parents and siblings)
- Career
- Spiritual
- Health
- Friends
- Community service
- Finances
- Adventure (things that bring fun and excitement to your life)
- Gardening
- Hobbies/crafts
- Education

What are the top ten domains of your life? Don't feel any need to stick to the examples in the previous list. And don't include a domain just because you want to look good or feel like people will judge you for omitting it. Be true to yourself. If you get stuck, flip back to the previous chapter where you discussed what matters to you. You're likely to spark an idea by looking over what you wrote there.

1. _____

2. _____

3. _____

4. _____

5. _____

6. _____

7. _____

8. _____

9. _____

10. _____

Got your ten domains figured out? Congratulations! This is a huge accomplishment. Gaining this kind of clarity about what matters to you is the key to building confidence and giving direction to your life.

Seeing the Future of the Ten Domains

Now, the next step is going to be difficult. You're going to select a domain of your life, flash-forward to five years from today (if today is November 4, 2014, you should be thinking about November 4, 2019), and then write in detailed language what you'll be experiencing on that day if that domain of your life is proceeding exactly like you want it to.

As you do this, you'll want to make your vision of each domain feel as real as possible. You don't just want to ponder things you'd like in five years' time; you want to wholly transport yourself to that day. Think about all of the details in the vision. Go through each of the five senses: What do you see around you? What does it smell like? What does it taste like? What do you hear? What can you touch, and what does it feel like?

For example, you might write about smelling the grape-fruit-scented candle while you're sitting in a comfortable brown leather sofa in your family room. It doesn't matter if you even own the brown leather sofa, but if it is the leather sofa you want to have in the future and that helps move you to five years from now, then make sure you include it in your writing. Or, you might write about lounging in the sitting room of your house on a lake just talking to your spouse or significant other enjoying the solace and the warm breeze in May. Again, the more you can feel it and describe it when you write it, the more this whole exercise will have life in it—the life you desire to have in the future.

The best way to do this is to write as if you were writing to a close friend you hadn't seen in five years. Imagine you are bringing them up to date on that domain of your life. You want to let yourself experience your future success without thoughts of limitations, boundaries, or obstacles. No self-criticism or negativity allowed.

Here are a few excerpts from my domains (though the full versions of most are over a page each):

Relationship with a Future Spouse

I am your helper. I am the one you wrap your arms around at night. I am the one who knows what is going through your mind just by looking into your eyes. I am the one who loves you unconditionally. You know me as the "rock," but you know me well and you know how much I really need you.

Notice the detail is about how the relationship works, there are no details about what the future spouse needs to look like and have; the focus is what allows two people to bond and support one another. Also, it is written from an "I" perspective since you can only control yourself, not the other person.

Career

I am a life coach now. My business is going quite well. I have more than enough clients. I help people reach their life dreams by holding them accountable to their promises. I am also doing some public speaking about being intentional with life. I have helped hundreds of clients, primarily professional Latina women with their life dreams. Many have achieved great things as a result of my coaching programs.

Notice I did not write about how I was going to get there or what I had to leave in order to get the career. This domain should reflect the type of career that aligns with your passion, what you would do if money were not issue. It should reflect what you would do even if you were not paid; you would do it for free because it is what you are yearning to do with your gifts and talents. Many would call this your passion.

Immediate Family

I am childless for the first time since my youngest daughter is now in college. My only son is in graduate school, and my oldest daughter just finished graduate school. It's just the dog and me. The kids come home when they can, always bringing home their laundry bags. We still all get together for Thanksgiving; it's our family tradition. I am a strong supporter and encourager for them now. I help them reach their dreams. They know I am always here for them. They see my faith in God and how he has provided for me all these years. My girls see me as a strong woman, a lioness. They know that they can do it alone if they have to because they saw me do it.

Notice the emphasis on the relationship component with the kids who are now adults. It focuses on what kind of support and connections exist within the family. Although it may include career aspirations for the kids, we really have no control over what they choose as their career, so don't get hung up on what they should be when they grow up. Stretch your imagination: who do you want to be for your children, whether they're young or adults?

Finances

We have successfully put three kids through college, allowing them to graduate debt-free. Additionally, my pension is secure and I have been able to invest wisely to ensure I can be comfortable when I retire. I plan to retire in my late fifties, so I know I have to set aside money to give me the lifestyle I want to have when I retire.

Notice the specificity around what needs to be in place to have the lifestyle I want to have. Be very specific in respect to the lifestyle you want to maintain and the financial goals that will help get you there.

A Few Notes Before You Get Started

Before you get to work on the ten domains exercise, I want to detour for just a moment and give you some thoughts on three commonly chosen domains: children, your relationship with your significant other, and community involvement/volunteering.

Relationship with Children

Children, if you have them, are obviously part of your family, but for the sake of this exercise, I recommend that you consider them a domain of their own, as I did in my list. Children— whether they're under the age of eighteen or adults—occupy tremendous space in our lives. When they're young, we are so entwined in the everyday routines of raising them and keeping them safe that it often feels like it will stay that way forever;

that can create anxiety and frustration. But since I have been there and am now on the other side, I can tell you that it is not forever. One day, they will leave you, and you will become an empty nester. The complexity of the phases of parenting calls for children to occupy their own domain.

Relationship with Spouse or Significant Other

Another category I want you to isolate from the family domain is your spouse or significant other—the most important person in your life. That person knows you better than anyone else, and spends more time with you than anyone (or at least I hope so). Your partner has seen the good, the bad, and the ugly, and yet continued to stand by your side. Because of the starring role this person plays in your life, he or she merits a separate domain in this phase of your Life Plan.

At the beginning of the relationship, the hours fly by, and you just can't get enough of your love; it's effortless. But as the years pass, it becomes easy to take the relationship for granted, and it can become vulnerable to complacency. Without warning, one day you wake up and your partner is a stranger. It takes effort to tend to a relationship and help it flourish.

My husband and I maintain a date night once a week as a priority even after eight years of marriage. The key to remember is that your children will all leave you one day, and the only person who will be sitting across the dinner table and riding in your car with you will be your spouse. Decide now to make your significant other a priority in your life and carve out a separate domain just for him or her.

Community Involvement/Volunteering

Many people select a domain that has to do with giving back to their community. As you know from my own story, I think this is a worthwhile pursuit. But if you decide to write about this domain in the following exercise, I want you to be very specific about what community you're serving and how.

If you're not specific enough and simply decide that "community involvement" or "volunteering" is important to you, you'll start to feel guilt every time you turn down an invitation to be involved in such a project. That's a big problem, because you'll quickly get overcommitted and frustrated. Time is finite, and you must use it wisely by volunteering only where your passion and skill match the activity. Everyone brings a unique gift to a cause, so find where your gift fits, and don't stretch yourself to the point of exhaustion.

When you know exactly how you want to volunteer and be involved in your community, you'll be able to turn down opportunities that aren't a good match without guilt. That's better for you and the people you're serving.

Exercise 5.2: Seeing Your Future, Domain by Domain

Now take a deep breath. It's your turn. On the next few pages, I want you to describe precisely what you want your life to be, domain by domain.

Don't rush through this exercise! Set aside an hour or two to start, but if fatigue sets in, stop and pick it up another day. Take your time, even if it takes you a couple of weeks to work through the exercise. It must be done with intentionality and complete honesty, so having a certain amount of energy as you write is key. Some clients have written one or two whole pages per domain; there's no limit on length.

Start by choosing the domain you're going to work on first. I suggest you start with the one that is currently challenging you the most at this moment in your life. For instance, if you have been struggling with a decision concerning your current job (such as whether to leave it or whether to ask for a promotion), then you should start with the career domain. Or if you are challenged with work-life balance and haven't spent much time alone with your spouse or significant other, which has caused you to be distant or short with one another, then the relationship domain is a good place to start.

You also have to move past the boundaries that usually hold you back when you set goals. Remove your limitations. Unshackle yourself. Don't think about whether you have the skills, the experience, the credentials, or anything else it will take to get to where you want to go. That doesn't mean I want you to write a series of pipe dreams, but I do want you to be true to what you want each domain to look like in five years, no matter how daunting or improbable it might seem to reach your desired destination.

I won't lie: as I said before, writing out your desires for the first couple of domains will be difficult. You're probably not used to thinking about yourself or your future in this way, and it takes some getting used to. But if you hit a block, forge ahead. Living intentionally requires hard work, and it must be done. As you move through the domains, you might find that you're getting better at writing down the limitless potential for each one; if so, loop back to the earlier domains and make additions as you see fit.

Domain 1   _____

Domain 2   _____

Domain 3   _____

Domain 4   _____

Domain 5 _____

Domain 6 _____

Domain 7 _____

Domain 8 _____

Domain 9 _____

Domain 10 _____

Once you've created a vision for all ten domains, go back and read what you wrote. Does it excite you? Does it terrify you? It should do both. Now read it again. Are your visions for the domains things you can accomplish just by continuing to do what you're already doing today? Did you, for example, envision yourself as VP of your company when you know that you're definitely on track to become VP? If so, then you aimed too low—you're still thinking too small. A bigger dream would be to reach for the executive vice president or senior vice president title.

I want you to make your dream big—so big, in fact, that it frightens you when you read it. I want you to have no idea, no clue, as to how you will accomplish your dream. If it's not scaring you at least a little bit, rewrite it to make it bigger.

Now I want to challenge you even further by asking you to read it to someone you trust to solicit a response from him or her as to whether or not your aim is small or if you really are choosing a bigger life. As you know, people are almost always willing to render an opinion about your life; but please make sure it is someone who will be willing to challenge you. Rewrite it based on that person's feedback.

Congratulations—writing all ten domains is a giant feat in creating a roadmap for your life! After you've come to final versions of all your domains, take another moment to read all ten of them in one sitting. As you read them, ask yourself whether you're feeling the following emotions:

- Clarity as to where you are going
- Peace of mind
- Belief in your vision
- Goals for your life (not just for your work)
- Love for life
- Intentionality
- Purpose
- Excitement
- Some fear

If you're having most or all of these feeling as you read your visions for the ten domains, you're on the right track toward the life you truly want to live.

Chapter 6

Making Your Life Plan a Reality

▶▶ I've been to a lot of graduation ceremonies in my life, and I'm always struck by how certain the keynote speakers seem that everyone in their young audience has a bright future ahead—and yet how vague they are on what it will take to get there. Usually the commencement address goes on about all the opportunities and great experiences these young adults will have, as if they're going to get up, grab their diplomas, and walk right into the life of their dreams.

But as these listeners will soon find out, that's almost never the case. I recently spoke with one young man at a college graduation lunch; he was moments away from hearing one of those very commencement speeches. He was a lanky guy, and my guess is that he was an extrovert. He seemed very comfortable speaking to everyone in the room. He spoke about holding a position of authority in his fraternity, and he had a lot of confidence in his ability to lead others. He frankly told me how he had messed up in his early school years—his grades had been less than stellar—but how he was now committed to studying hard, working at the school, and leading his fraternity. And yet, as he told me about how hard he'd worked to pay his way through school and explained that he hoped to land an accounting job, I could sense uncertainty in his voice.

"I don't have any set plans yet, but I know I'll get there," he told me, the unspoken "*one day*" hanging in the air. He was ambitious, looking forward to the future, and yet his fear of the unknown was palpable.

It wasn't my place to stand there and tell him how to live his life, but I knew this young man had some work to do if he wanted to make his dream come true. He'd have to take his "maybe someday" attitude and replace it with a clear roadmap to show him where to go. Without that, he had only hope and good luck to drive him forward—neither of which is reliable without a plan to follow.

When you first picked up this book, maybe you were like this graduate, hoping for a bright future but not sure what it looked like or how you'd get there. The good news is that you've moved on from that place!

Your Life Plan, the written statement of where you want to be—physically, mentally, relationally, developmentally, spiritually, and financially—in the future is your blueprint, your inspiration to move you toward the life you really want to have.

This is a giant feat. Perhaps it's not entirely clear what steps you need to take to get to the ideal expressed in the Life Plan, but you don't need to map out every single baby step along the way. The vision itself is your roadmap. When you're stuck on what to do next, immerse yourself in sensations you evoked in the Life Plan, and you'll usually generate ideas on how to take yourself one step closer.

Now that you've taken lingering thoughts and the desires of your heart and declared them on paper, you can see what you want for your future. You can no longer rely on the words "I don't know what I want"—because now you do know. The markers you've set for the future will help you tackle uncertainty and will give you a course to navigate.

As you navigate this course, there are times you'll suddenly feel lost. You'll lose sight of where you are going, and discouragement will set in. But because you've created a Life Plan, all you have to do is simply set your eyes on the upcoming markers and move ahead with confidence. The life you've designed awaits you. And that, my friend, will pull you forward.

Before we move on and discuss some tools you can use to start moving toward your vision of the future, let's look at a few brief examples of how establishing a Life Plan can change lives.

Paula's Health Domain

From the day I first met her, I knew Paula had a heart of gold. She first came to me as a client several years ago, and she charmed me right away with her contagious positivity. In our first session together, Paula explained that throughout her life, she always had to be the achiever. She had to get the best grades in school, always had to take the more difficult path so she could prove to everyone that she could do it despite the challenge.

Despite her cheerful nature, Paula hadn't been able to extend much positivity to herself in recent years, and she felt like she'd fallen into a deep rut in her life. In addition to questioning her need to always be the best, Paula was struggling with another adversary that dated back to her childhood: her weight. She was now severely overweight, and I could see in her eyes that her physical condition burdened her, emotionally and bodily. So it didn't surprise me when she established "Health" as one of her domains. I was happy that she had chosen to work on her health; I knew she felt that this unconquered problem was an important starting point for her. But what she said next *did* surprise me: "I want to run a marathon," she said, looking somewhere between sheepish at admitting such a lofty goal and stubbornly determined to make it happen.

I questioned her a bit more and found that this was something she'd wanted to do for a long time. Once she'd worked up the courage to declare it in her Life Plan, I—as her coach—had to hold her accountable to her commitment. Paula's first step was brave: spurred on by her vivid description of what it would feel like to finish that first marathon, she signed up to run a 5K, set a target pace, and hired a running coach to help her train. She also told her friends and family that she was going to run a marathon.

Flash-forward two years: Paula had lost a significant amount of weight and completed several races. Her eyes were still set on running the full marathon—at or before the five-year mark. She'd even sustained her commitment to the goal despite a running injury that took her off the track for a couple of months. Paula's five years aren't quite up, but I know without a doubt that she will run her marathon by then.

I was so inspired by Paula's determination and progress that I made an addition to the Health domain of my own Life Plan: a vision of one day running a full marathon myself. I've now run several 5Ks and one 8K, and I'm registered for my first half marathon. Every other day, as I train—with the concrete hitting the soles of my feet, the aches and pains screaming at me to stop—I envision hitting that finish line, exhausted but elated, and knowing that I reached what I set my eyes on achieving. I picture having overcome every negative thought, having silenced every little voice that told me, "You don't have to do this running thing, Luz. It really doesn't mean much." When I'm able to push down that negativity, even during an excruciating run, it's because I've drawn on the power my Life Plan has given me and accepted that I do not have to live my life bound by routines that don't move me forward.

In the near future, both Paula and I will break through that tape at the finish line, just as we're breaking through our limiting routines in pursuit of our Life Plans.

India's Career Domain

India was another one of my clients, and she had dreamed for years of being a doctor. At first glance, she appeared to be very meek. She spoke with a quiet, gentle voice that matched her stature: she was about five feet tall and couldn't have weighed more than one hundred pounds. But, upon getting to know her, I saw that India possessed an intense passion for helping mentally ill people.

Becoming a physician and helping these patients had been her heart's desire ever since her mother was diagnosed with schizophrenia—an ordeal that affected India's entire family. She had painful memories of her mother being incapacitated or gone from the home for weeks at a time. She'd been too young to realize that these absences happened because her mother had to be periodically hospitalized. All little India knew was that something was wrong with her mom and that she could do nothing to help her. As she grew up and realized the extent of her mother's illness, India experienced guilt and regret: she felt like she could have helped her parents cope had she understood the situation.

When I met India, she had completed her undergraduate education and was just beginning to think about medical school. She spoke of it often, but she just couldn't believe that she could one day really be a doctor. She tended to focus on the barriers—finances were a big one, but even bigger was her learning disability. India didn't know how she was going to pass the MCAT given her condition, and it became a big stumbling block to reaching her dream.

As I worked with India on her Life Plan, I saw that without a doubt she wanted to become a doctor; we therefore focused her coaching sessions on how she would get there. As we created her Life Plan in the Career domain, India slowly began to believe that it was attainable. Invigorated by her five-year vision, she took steps like studying for the MCAT and applying to medical schools. She also addressed her learning disability and applied for the special processes that granted her adequate time to take the test.

When India took the MCAT shortly thereafter, she passed. She was blown away by her achievement. She got into medical school, is now finishing her residency, and will soon fulfill one of the most crucial domains of her Life Plan by becoming a doctor.

India was one of my very first clients, and her success is one of the reasons I launched my coaching practice—and a big part of why I believe in the power of the Life Plan.

My Life Plan

When I wrote my first Life Plan, I was divorced and not quite ready for the idea of getting remarried. When I wrote my Relationship domain, it was about a marriage to a man I hadn't even met yet. I didn't write about what he would look like or what he had; instead, I wrote about the type of person he was and how our relationship would function.

Two years after I wrote that domain, I met the man who is now my husband. Now, it didn't happen magically; he didn't just show up and knock at my door one day. I had to first believe that I would be married again. Moreover, I had to come to terms with even wanting to be married again after such a painful first marriage. The Life Plan helped me do both those things.

But that wasn't enough—I had to take action, to put myself out there. I had my own coach at the time, and she helped me act even when I resisted. She held me accountable to my Relationship domain by asking me to take baby steps to put myself out there in the world of dating. Even though I'd warmed up to the idea of seeing people again and maybe even getting married, I hadn't done much to get there. During one session, my coach saw that I'd taken no action in the Relationship domain and became frustrated with me.

"Is finding a husband a real priority to you?" she asked firmly. It was as if she'd taken me by the shoulders and given me a good shake. This *was* my biggest priority, and I had to do something about it.

Social media seemed to be a safe place to begin, so I joined a dating service. Two months into the process, a gentleman with the service, who had interviewed me, recommended that I meet one of his other interviewees. I met the guy and, well, we married one year later and have been married nine years now.

I know that my Life Plan—and prodding from my coach to carry it out—led to my marriage. Putting a vision of my relationship down on paper was a commitment to the world, but mostly to me. The process worked, and I met the man of my dreams!

And as I wrote about earlier in this book, the Life Plan has helped me make other achievements. It helped me move away from a career that no longer fulfilled me to start my own successful coaching practice. As it comes time to revisit my Life Plan for the next five years, I revere it as a powerful tool that will move me toward the life I truly want to live.

But enough about me. What about you? Since you now hold your Life Plan in your hand, you're probably thinking about ways you can begin to move toward your dreams and achieve some of the successes I've described. This is easier said than done—as always, labels and judgments will be eager to hold you back—but there are many steps you can take to keep you moving toward your dreams. Here are several to get you started.

1. **Create a Vision Board**. The Vision Board is a visual representation of your Life Plan. It's a handy tool, since you can place it prominently in your home or office so that you're constantly reminded of where your path is leading you. We'll discuss the Vision Board in more detail in the next chapter.

2. **Check your language**. It's vital that you believe in your plan, but that's virtually impossible if you talk about "if" you achieve such-and-such thing instead of "when" you achieve it. This simple shift in how you speak will make you a believer in your own Life Plan, and it will encourage others to support you and hold you accountable.

    I am a compulsive planner, currently using three calendars plus my iPhone calendar. You might think that's a bit obsessive, but my calendars are important because they tell me what I am doing next. The language you use to talk about your Life Plan serves the same function. You must begin to use language that moves you toward the next thing. There cannot be any doubt about what's ahead, which is what "if" implies. Even if you don't have a clue as to how you are going to get there, the language you use must express confidence in your Life Plan.

Try it right now, out loud. First say, "If I achieve _____." Sit with it for a moment and see how it feels. Now say, "When I achieve _____." Can you already feel yourself moving toward the goal? In the battle of "if" versus "when," when always wins.

3. **Incorporate action steps into your calendar or "to do" list.** Your weekly planner, your monthly planner, and your "to do" list can all help you establish steps that move you toward your Life Plan. Remember—even though this is a five-year plan, you need to start taking action now.

I put reminders about my next action steps on my monthly calendar, using an abbreviation that helps me remember all my domains: the 5 Fs, plus Me. **F**aith is for my Spiritual domain, and **F**amily is for domains relating to my husband, my immediate family, and my extended family. The third, fourth, and fifth Fs are the **F**riends domain, the **F**inance domain (which captures career), and the **F**ellowship domain (which captures volunteer work and community support). Finally, there's the "Me" domain which includes my health, travel, hobbies, adventures, and "me" time.

Each month, I write the 5 Fs plus Me in the margins of my calendar and then write the actions I will take that month to move me toward my Life Plan. For example, in the month of May under Family, I might write down that I need to take time to celebrate six birthdays in the month, including my own. Last May, I also wrote that I needed to take time to celebrate two of my children's graduations. These actions are about more than acknowledging the events; they are about being present and intentional around these family members, as written in my Life Plan. By writing down the 5 Fs plus Me on the calendar each month, I am reminding myself to live my life that month in a way that walks me toward my Life Plan.

I recommend writing down at least one action step for each of your domains each month. That way, you are checking in each month on your Life Plan. Of course, you can have as many steps as you want, but don't overwhelm yourself by putting down too many.

4. **Review your Life Plan monthly**. Thirty days flies by. Just think about the past New Year's Day. It seemed like a whole new year stretched out far into the distance, right? But then all of sudden, winter passes and then spring. Suddenly summer is at your backdoor, followed quickly by fall.

   Given the rapid pace of life—and the fact that so much can change in thirty days—I recommend you revisit your Life Plan every month. If you can do it weekly or biweekly, even better, but the minimum should be once a month. During your review, assess whether you have taken any action toward your Life Plan. Recommit to taking action if you haven't, and congratulate yourself if you have. Then start figuring out what the next steps are that will move you a little further down the road. Whatever you do, don't start second-guessing the plan you wrote. Charge ahead instead.

5. **Hire a coach**. As you saw in my story earlier in this chapter, my coach was instrumental in helping me stay committed

to my Life Plan. You may find you also need this external support. Family and friends are great, but sometimes there's nothing like having a neutral third party whose job it is to keep you motivated and accountable. The financial investment is worth it.

As someone who's been a coach for over eleven years, I have helped hundreds of people take action in their lives— people who were either stuck or afraid or truly uncommitted to taking any time or action toward something they really wanted for their life. That is the role of coaches; they hold your dreams in their hands until you believe in them yourself. When you hire them, they commit to help you achieve things; good coaches will not accept mediocrity and will not let you give up on your dreams. It is an incredibly powerful relationship, unlike any other in your life.

The International Coaching Federation (*www.coach federation.org*) is the best organization in the world that trains and credentials coaches. And, of course, you can always contact me directly for coaching services—see the final page of this book for my information.

6. **Make declarations of the life you really want to have**. If you do not declare your Life Plan to anyone but yourself, you are likely to fail. But when you publicly declare what you intend to do, you create accountability and increase your chances of success. We don't like to let others down, so our word to others is a powerful driving force.

The notion of declaration has been a difficult one for several of my clients because they are afraid to be seen as a failure if they don't achieve what they declared they would. These feelings likely stem from our belief that we shouldn't promise anything we know we may not achieve. When we give in to that pressure, we live our lives in a very small and safe way so that we don't disappoint others—or ourselves.

In chapter 2, when I was describing the "transformational coaching" sessions that introduced me to many of the ideas in this book, I mentioned a young man who made a public declaration that AIDS would be obliterated. *Wow, I remember thinking, is that guy nuts?* But over time, my attitude changed. Every time I heard him make that declaration, I believed him more and wanted to help him achieve his dream.

Similarly, President John F. Kennedy declared that we were going to the moon, even before a spacecraft had been built that could get there! There is tremendous power in declarations, so learn to overcome your own fears and let go of what others may think if you fail. You will see a marked difference in your walk toward your Life Plan.

7. **Use your Life Plan to help you make decisions**. Many opportunities will come your way in life, but they won't all get you closer to where you want to go. That's why it's important to use your Life Plan as a measuring stick and evaluate whether certain choices you plan to make align with your vision of the future.

I was recently on vacation and, on one free afternoon, was whisked away in a golf cart to take a tour of the resort. As it turned out, the tour was really a timeshare presentation where my husband and I would be shown a villa and vacation choices in five thousand cities. We had recently been discussing future vacations with our mostly adult children, so we didn't leave when we realized this was a pitch; we thought the tour would be worth our time.

The tour of the villa was spectacular—pools, beautiful

furniture, private decks, chefs who would make amazing meals, you name it. We started visualizing ourselves there with our children sitting around the private pool just having a good time. The package included thirty-nine years of vacations, so when the agent presented the price tag of $65,000, it didn't sound too bad. We were driven by our desire to find ways to bring our family together in the future, and since we had already experienced such a trip with about ten family members the year before, we were caught up in the moment. The temptation to say yes was overwhelming, but then my husband and I stopped and asked ourselves, "Does this fit in our current Financial domain?"

It pained me to admit it, but the answer was a clear no. Our Financial domain did not include taking on more debt, and purchasing the villa would impact our Financial domain and several other domains in our Life Plan. Of course, the agent wasn't happy about losing a sale that day, but we breathed a sigh of relief as we walked away—absolutely sure we had made the right decision. Later that weekend, we overheard a couple say they had just purchased a villa, and there was no jealousy on our part. We simply breathed a sigh of relief that we were still on our path to our Life Plan.

8. **Use your Life Plan Checklist to define steps you will take on a weekly basis.** The weekly Checklist (see the appendix) is a simple template that's useful for tracking progress on a weekly basis. It is a very useful bite-size approach toward reaching your five-year Life Plan. As you can see, the Checklist gives you a place to write all your domains and then establish a task for the week in each one, along with an overall intention for the week. Every week, I use this to set intentional actions I will take toward my Life Plan.

There is enough space for several steps under each domain. I like the Checklist because, like my many calendars, it is a visual of my commitments.

That's eight tools—a bit much to try at once. Start out by trying a combination of two or three of them until you figure out what works best for you. You may find that you can make some of them habits, so that they're constantly running in the background while you focus on others. Adjust your use of these tools accordingly so that the process of moving toward your Life Plan becomes natural and exciting to you. Keep your eyes on your plan. Soon, you will begin to feel your confidence rise, and you'll start to see the possibilities for bringing your life-design into reality.

I believe you can do it—do you?

Chapter 7

The Vision Board

▶▶ At some point, all us have set out with a plan to change our lives and failed. In fact, it sometimes feels like *most* of our attempts in this arena fail. Maybe we got too busy. Maybe our priorities changed. Maybe we just forgot what our goal was, day by day by day.

It's extremely easy to lose momentum, especially when you're pushing yourself out of ruts and routines and emerging into the frightening, uncomfortable world of change. As you start executing your Life Plan, you're going to feel inertia at times. You're going to want to give up and fall back into your comfortable routine.

One of the tools mentioned in the previous chapter—the Vision Board—is particularly helpful for keeping you on track. I know it's a cliché, but it's true: a picture is worth a thousand words. When you can actually see a visual representation of the five-year goals in each of your life domains, your motivation will be stronger and more immediate. On the board, your goals for your future coalesce into a creative representation of where you want to be in five years—and it will make that future feel visceral, achievable, and almost inevitable.

The basics of creating a Vision Board are easy, but you might feel resistance from yourself as you choose and arrange the images. Push through it. Keep going. Get your first version made and understand that you can tweak it later.

Let's walk through the steps of the Vision Board process:

1. Begin by **purchasing your materials**. The foundation will be a large piece of poster board. Any color that inspires you is fine—I found one with a refreshing blue sky and clouds on it. The other essential items are a pair of scissors, an assortment of markers, and some glue.

   But you don't have to stop there. If it feels right, consider getting creative with your supplies. Go anywhere scrapbooking materials are sold and look for stickers, borders, staples, glitter, or ribbons. Let your inner artist out!

2. Next, **divide your board into domains**. Go back to your domain exercise and mark out a place on the board for each one. You can organize this however you want—some people prefer a neat grid, while others like a looser, more nebulous approach. It's up to you. Often, people will choose to put their most important domain smack-dab in the middle.

3. Now it's time to **collect your pictures**. You're going to look for quick visual reminders that represent the essence of your Life Plan and your dreams for where you'll be in five years for each domain of your life.

   A natural place to start is with pictures of family and friends for these respective domains. Then look for images that correspond to all the other areas of your Life Plan. Look through that stack of old magazines, or get on Google Image Search and fire up your printer.

   If one of your domains is Health, be on the lookout for

pictures of wholesome food, of exercise equipment, of gym shoes, of healthy-looking people, or of yourself from a healthier time in your life. You might also choose to add words: "Marathon," for example.

4.   When you have several images and words selected for each domain, you can **start constructing the board**. Start with one domain. Cut out and trim your pictures, and paste them in the relevant spot on the board. There are no hard and fast rules, but before you attach each image or word to the board, ask yourself, *Does this inspire me? Does it fit with my five-year plan?* If you hesitate, it comes off. Repeat the process for each domain.

5.   Once you have all the domains filled out on the Vision Board, step away from it for at least a day. Then come back and **reassess your work**. Pull your domain exercise back out and take a spin through the board, ensuring that your work accurately reflects the vision you had. If you find something isn't quite right, start tweaking.

6.   Now, **post the Vision Board somewhere you can see it**. Your work on the project is only worth anything if you look at the board on a daily basis. Don't put it in the corner of the laundry room or in a utility closet. You want it front and center, in a place where you'll see it every day.

   Each day, try to stop and meditate on the board for at least a couple of minutes. Let yourself feel excited about the future. Let yourself envision achieving all the things you've collected. Feel that this *is* your future, and that it's only a matter of time until you get there.

7. Finally, **share your Vision Board with trusted friends and family**. This is another way of declaring your Life Plan and holding yourself accountable. When you open yourself up and share your desires with the people you love, you'll find that they'll almost always support you. And it's so much easier to make progress when you know you're not going it alone.

As you examine your completed Vision Board, which resulted from your written Life Plan, give yourself a pat on your back. This is a great accomplishment. You now have a roadmap for your next five years. Most people do not have this, so you've officially joined the ranks of those who choose to live their life intentionally. Welcome!

Final Thoughts

Years ago, I was coaching one of my husband's best friends. This man is a deep thinker—he is curious about every aspect of life. In each conversation I had with him, he seemed eager to strike out on new paths and discover fresh possibilities for his future.

We worked through his domains, developed his vision for what they each looked like in five years, and discussed his first steps for achieving his Life Plan. A few months after we'd completed this work, he asked me a somewhat difficult question: Could he alter his five-year Life Plan?

My response was simple: if you were completely honest at the time you wrote the five-year plan, there should be no need to alter it. Perhaps that sounds a little harsh, but if we allow ourselves to constantly edit and reedit our vision of where we want to be in five years, the exercise loses some of its power. Our priorities shift, the steps we take toward our goals change, and we lose focus. That makes it more likely that we'll slip back into fearful, routine-driven living.

That said, life is unpredictable. Whether it's a chance encounter that leads to love or a shattering diagnosis, all of us get curveballs that change our lives, sometimes in major ways. When that happens, it does sometimes become necessary to tweak your Life Plan.

Here's an example from my life. When I first laid out the financial domain of my Life Plan, I set an ambitious goal that was nevertheless achievable given the economic climate. But then September 2008 happened. The economy took a nosedive, and over the course of the rest of that year and most of 2009, we saw a full-fledged crash. I, like so many Americans, watched my 401(k) drop, and I realized I was living in a new reality. The recession meant that there was no way I could meet my five-year goal. But instead of beating myself up, I accepted that this was a situation outside of my control, made an allowance for a slight tweak of my Life Plan, and moved forward undeterred.

There was no way I could've seen that coming, so I categorized it as a necessary and acceptable change to the Life Plan. But to avoid having to go back and make too many alterations, it's best not to include goals in your five-year plan that aren't primarily under your control. For example, if you write that you want to see your son in medical school in five years, there's a good chance you'll end up having to make a revision. What if, three years down the road, your son decides instead to go to law school or culinary school, or to pursue a career in business? It would be foolish to try to change his mind just so you could keep your original plan alive. Instead, try having a vision of your son happy in his career in five years. Don't be so specific as to picture him in a particular type of school or job; instead, cultivate a vision of him excitedly telling you about his studies, whatever the subject may be.

But what if your daughter decides to get married and suddenly you have a new son-in-law as part of the family domain? What if your sister has a child and you're a new aunt? Of course, that's another form of change that's not under your control. You should be able to make these additions to the family domain without changing the essence of this part of your Life Plan. If you wrote your Life Plan in a general enough manner, you don't even need to add the new person in; you can simply extend your plan to include them without an official change.

The Life Plan is a roadmap that will help you achieve your life dreams, but it doesn't need to contain every single detail of how you're going to get there. The plan is a vision, not a script. It is meant to serve you, not to enslave you by demanding a stream of updates and revisions. If you wrote your Life Plan with honesty after plenty of serious thought, its core components shouldn't change, no matter what happens on the road to achieving it.

I wrote my very first Life Plan on November 24, 2001. It included the domains of family, spiritual, soul mate, community, career, extended family, education, friends, and home. Did I meet everything I wrote about in each of those domains? Of course not, but I did accomplish living my life toward the design I had created.

For example, I wrote in my community domain that I was going to be involved in the church's camp with the children, but that never happened. Instead, later in 2005, I found myself involved with the children of the church on Friday nights for three years with my husband. The results were different than what I had planned, but I did end up working with the children from the church. Another example of a departure from my plan was the career domain, which was mostly about being a full-time, self-employed life coach. Well, I did become a coach, but I had to do it part time at first, since I—a single mother—had to provide for my family. But much later, in 2009, I was finally able to pursue my passion for coaching full time.

I'm telling you this because I want to leave you with an important point: the Life Plan sets your direction, and your destination may not look precisely like the visions you wrote down or the images you pasted on your Vision Board. In the grand scheme of things, that hardly matters. The important thing is that the Life Plan sets you on the right path and jolts you out of the routine-driven existence you led before. It helps you live with intention and leads you to what you really want in ways you didn't even imagine were possible.

Since making my first Life Plan, I've been through two other rounds of this exercise. In the second round, I invited my new husband to partake in the process with me—it became a "we" focus rather than a "me" focus. We even designed a Vision Board together, one that combines the essences of our separate written Life Plans. I can truly say that this served us well. At one point, we found ourselves falling into an out-of-focus way of living. My husband had become self-employed and was working hard to build his own company. I wanted to support him in this endeavor, so the business started taking up much of my time, too. Soon, the dates on our calendar nearly all revolved around his work, and the discussions we usually had to sync ourselves stopped happening. Routines had taken over again.

As soon as we realized we were getting off track, we sat down with our Vision Board to revisit our dream and commitments. Immediately, we booked one of the many vacations we had on the Vision Board, even though it meant carving out precious time on our very busy calendars and using the money we had set aside for vacation. And this year, to keep us moving toward our five-year vision of running a full marathon, we signed up to do a half-marathon.

As I write these words, we have three years left on our current plan. The Vision Board is on the wall of my office. I see it nearly every day, and some days I sit a while and revisit it.

I am not stressed about the future and what it holds for me. I know I don't have full control of my destiny, but I know I've pointed myself in the right direction, and that gives me peace. This year I turned fifty-five, and it was no big deal. I didn't stress like when I turned forty, when I thought, *I can't believe I am forty!* and had a series of questions about what lay ahead of me and questioned whether I had achieved all that I planned to achieve—all the silly questions we dream up to make our lives seem purposeful. I have learned that there is no boundary line—like reaching forty, fifty, or sixty—that delineates our purpose; on the contrary, life is about the breaths we take every day. I wake up each morning thankful for the day, thankful for health, thankful for air conditioning and indoor plumbing and all the things that make my life function. I try to live in the present each day, directed by my calendars but being open to the unplanned interruptions that cross my path.

Of course, there are bad days. But when they occur, I have to go to my tried-and-true practices to energize me and keep me calm—things like praying, reading inspirational stories, watching inspirational videos, or talking about what I'm feeling with people I trust and who know me. In fact, I just had one of those bad days; it began with a 5:30 a.m. call from my husband, who had just had a major car accident. Our car was totaled. I could've felt upset, but I set an intention of focusing my attention on where it should be: Don was fine and the person who hit him was fine. As the day progressed, I found myself increasingly grateful for the fact that he was alive—and, well, the car can be replaced. We handled the situation with calmness: going to the hospital, getting a rental car, making the necessary phone calls; there was an eerie calmness to the day. We hugged more than usual that day, and we spent more time together that evening, because we were reminded once again that the road of life has twists and turns, so you'd better be prepared to shift accordingly.

Worry, anger, fear—these are emotions that don't serve anyone well, so it is my goal in life to get rid of these just as soon as they show up. I focus on the positives instead, and that always works. This year, I got a small blackboard as a gift from a dear friend, and it says, "Today I am Grateful for" and then there is room for me to write. I hung that board in my office, and when I think of something or someone I'm thankful for, I just pick up the chalk and write. That little board serves to remind me that we should be grateful for something every day. Once again, there is power in writing it down.

When I begin to coach a new client, they're often focused more on their fear of the future than on gratefulness. I usually hear a lot of the uncertainty about their life, and often the words "I am stuck" are spoken. But those words are music to my ears, because that is when I know I can help them. This is the area I am gifted in, and I thrive on helping others find out how they can get unstuck.

I feel lucky to have gotten myself unstuck so I can do this work, and it's all thanks to intentional living. I find that I have a lot of peace around my future, because I can see it not only on paper and my Vision Board but also in my language. I feel like I am moving toward the life I was meant to live, and that brings me joy. Were someone to ask me where I want to be in five years, I wouldn't stress or struggle to answer. It's a no-brainer. I simply pull out my Life Plan and Vision Board, and the conversation begins.

Appendix

The Life Plan Checklist

Designing Your Life Plan

Title: <u>*Achieving Your Five-Year Plan*</u>

Client: <u>*(You)*</u>

Week: _____

Intention for the Week: _____

Domain 1	Domain 2	Domain 3

Domain 4	Domain 5	Domain 6

Appendix

Designing Your Life Plan

Title: *Achieving Your Five-Year Plan*

Client: *(You)*

Week:

Intention for the Week: _____

Domain 7

Domain 8

Domain 9

Domain 10

You

Others

Luz N. Canino-Baker, MBA

Luz Canino-Baker has a passion for seeing everyone perform at his or her full potential. After a successful twenty-eight year banking career, she started her own business in 2007, LNC Coaching, LLC. She coaches in excess of one hundred clients a year, and her core services include executive/life coaching and leadership development programs, and she puts on an annual professional development conference for Latinas, known as Latinas on the Plaza. In 2010, she joined the speaker circuit on the topics of work-life balance, branding yourself, and empowering employee resource groups. She is certified in Myers Briggs and Insights Discovery and will be certified in Emotional Intelligence in the fall of 2013. She holds a professional coaching certification from the International Academy of Behavioral Medicine, Counseling and Psychotherapy, Inc. and has applied for certification from the International Coaching Federation.

Ms. Canino-Baker spent the greater part of her career in banking at First National Bank of Chicago/Bank One; now JPMorgan Chase. There she had a successful 28-year career in commercial banking, corporate trust, investment management, and commercial credit card. After participating in an executive transformational coaching program, she was selected to coach and develop ten leaders in the Investment Management Group.

Ms. Canino-Baker served as the managing director of programs and marketing for the Hispanic Alliance for Career Enhancement (HACE) in Chicago. HACE is a national organization that serves a Latino constituency of 35,000 in Chicago, Houston, Los Angeles, Miami, and New York. She is also the founder of the Mujeres de HACE program, a leadership program for Latinas, which has to date graduated over 250 Latina leaders.

Ms. Canino-Baker holds a bachelor of science degree in management from DePaul University and an MBA from the University of Chicago. She is also an adjunct professor at DePaul University, National-Louis University, Benedictine University, and Lake Forest Graduate School of Management. She serves on the board of Harper College Educational Foundation, and on the advisory board of Uhlich Children's Advantage Network (UCAN). Her current memberships are: University of Chicago Business Women, National Society of Hispanic MBAs, National Hispanic Sales Network, and ALPFA.

Ms. Canino-Baker was selected by Chicago United as one of Chicago's Business Leaders of Color in 2007. In 2009, she was by recognized as one of Top 100 Under 50 by Diversity MBA Magazine. She is a graduate of the Boardroom Bound® Boardology™ Institute and profiled in the group's national director-candidate database. Luz is married to Don Baker, who is president of Stare Down the Lion Consulting. They live in Clarendon Hills as a blended family of five. *Designing Your Life Plan* is her first book.

Contact Luz

Luz Canino-Baker
luzcaninobaker@me.com
www.lnccoaching.com

CPSIA information can be obtained at www.ICGtesting.com
Printed in the USA
LVOW05s0748301113

363195LV00004B/9/P